The Icehouse Gang

MY YEAR WITH THE BLACK HAWKS

BRD

●

CHANDLER W. STERLING

CHARLES SCRIBNER'S SONS
New York

A–9.72(H)

Printed in the United States of America
Library of Congress Catalog Card
Number 72–1223
SBN 684–13040–8 (cloth)

Acknowledgments

Thanks and appreciation are due several persons for their part in helping me put together this story. Chief among them are Don Murphy, Director of Public Relations for the Chicago Black Hawks, and his staff, especially John Peters and Ed Walsh who had every right to avoid me from time to time when I was asking what I have come to learn were some dumb questions. The understanding, patience, and cooperation of all three of these persons were marked.

Several members of the press were of great assistance, especially Ted Damata and Bob Verdi of the Chicago *Tribune,* Dan Moulton of *Chicago Today,* and George Vass of the Chicago *Daily News.* Not once did any of these sports reporters let on that I was being a nuisance and sometimes a deterrent in their assignments with my constant interruptions. They taught me much.

I am also indebted to John Halligan of the New York Rangers and Joe Kadlec of the Philadelphia Flyers for making it possible for me to have access to both arenas including all privileges and hospitalities.

Whenever I found it more convenient to watch the game from the organ loft at the Chicago Stadium I was always welcomed by Al Melgard, the staff organist at the stadium since 1929. I finally came around to Al's way of thinking in selection of music for the final pieces to be played as the crowd filed out of the stadium and the teams disappeared into the dressing rooms. Consistently he selected "The Lord's Prayer" and sometimes "Good Night, My Someone." Inasmuch as there is usually a winner and a loser of every game the former was always appropriate although I could never totally accept the theology of the latter nor its place in an arena. However, I do owe Al thanks for his kindness and hospitality.

Lastly, my gratitude to the members of the Black Hawk Hockey Club for their expressions of interest, friendship, and trust. Without exception they went out of their way to make my job easier for me to do. If I start naming names here I would have to arrange them alphabetically and take ex-

Acknowledgments

treme care that none were omitted, for my debt is to all of them including those anonymous rookies who showed up for training camp and then went their way to play minor league and wait for next year's opportunity.

C.W.S.

Hilltown, Pennsylvania
January 28, 1972

Contents

Preface

There will never be a "paper iceman." Amateurs have survived the experience of professional play in football, baseball, and golf. It is remotely possible that someone may emerge to write about what it is like to play professional basketball, but such a feat will never be accomplished in professional ice hockey.

After a year with the Chicago Black Hawks I cannot imagine anyone but a fool even trying it. It would be suicide or at least leave permanent injury. No coach with a trace of humanity left in him would allow that kind of "rookie" to suit up and go out on the ice.

It takes eighteen years of skating experience and practice to produce a rookie in the National Hockey League. At least 13,000 hours are required to make a professional hockey player. One starts down the long road to the hockey big time at the age of three or four. The aspiring candidate had also better be able to skate at twenty miles an hour and be able to withstand even an accidental collision at the impact speed of forty mph. With less training, experience, and talent, I doubt very much if a writer-fan could avoid painful and possibly permanent injury even if the players were thoughtful of him—and don't count on that. If any man would be foolish enough to skate onto the ice during training camp with the regulars as well as the hungry and highly competitive rookies, I seriously doubt if he would be able to skate off the ice. He would likely make his exit horizontally and feetfirst.

This has nothing whatever to do with the alleged savagery of either the game or the players. It is simply that any skater with inferior skills, talent, discipline, or experience would not be able to protect himself in the fastest game in the world. Even angels would fear to skate on the thin ice of a training camp for any National Hockey League team. Being neither angel nor fool I restricted my time on the ice for after the workout when there were never more than three or four nice young men skating round and round. They were very kind to me. I was hardly a threat to them. Wisely restricting my skating to these quiet hours I survived to tell the story of the remarkable experience I had in becoming friends with these men who make their living playing a truly dangerous game. If a book requires a dedication to anyone, there could be but one person for that honor for a book such as this. That person is Everyman—every man who has ever played big league hockey, the ones who play the game year after year because it is The Game and because it is what they do best. No matter the exploitation of talent and manipulation of men, for even these are increasingly endured as this sport tightens up in the American philosophy of competition for the dollar. "Everyman" stays on in spite of these encroachments on personhood and his comparatively poor pay for the risks involved and the limited life expectancy of his playing days.

This is the story of men on thin ice. They are you and they are me, for all of us battle the odds on uncertain ground. In them we may see the order that may be lacking in our lives. Out there on the ice the issues are clear-cut. The contender not only knows what must be done but most frequently accomplishes what he sets out to do in spite of all interferences from the Enemy. In him we witness the achievement of purpose when he and his colleagues cope with constant crisis during that brief hour of the game. As spectators, we pay well to see men do well and thus restore something intangible to us that we don't seem to be capable of acquiring.

Bear in mind that they are not only talented athletes whose grace and courage it is a pleasure to witness but that they are men, not robots; persons, not pawns; living souls, not muscle machines. They, too, know and experience justice and injustice, the bitterness of defeat and the joy of victory, even as you and I. As do all men, they know what it feels like to be trapped into a corner and slammed up against the boards of life. They also know what it is like to be free.

The Icehouse Gang

1

What Am I Doing Here?

●

The mist slowly enveloped my body, encasing me. As I gazed across the ice from the center face-off circle where I was standing, I saw a solitary figure appear at the player's gate beyond the east goal. Wearing full pads and the bright red uniform of the Chicago Black Hawks and carrying his hockey stick, he began skating rhythmically around the outer orbit of the arena. He paid no attention to me. I don't believe that he saw me in the mist that swirled about him as his body became heated.

Outside, the September temperature was in the steaming high 80's. In the center of this cavernous icehouse, I was one of two lonely figures in this empty arena of the gladiators. Watching the skater go around and around in his solitude, I forgot my feet freezing in summer shoes. He continued to make his endless circles and swoops—a hawk slowly cutting lazy circles in his inverted sky. He, too, was now haloed.

This was Stan Mikita.

Winter and summer collided in the Chicago Stadium today. The lonely skater's summer sins of ease and relaxation had caught up with him today. He was skating backward into time as far as last April and the Stanley Cup finals. "It's mostly a matter of wind," Stan puffed as he pulled up momentarily into the center circle.

He scooped up some ice flakes created by his sudden stop. Balancing the slush on the blade of his stick, he suddenly turned and dumped it on my head as he skated back into his lonely orbit. As in *The Loneliness of the Long Distance Runner,* so it was here.

"All I knew was that you had to skate, skate, skate, without knowing why, really, you were skating. But on you went around and around, suddenly stopping and skating off in the opposite direction, around and in front of the goal net that made you afraid, around and around without knowing you'd been around. And banging men into the boards and colliding with an opponent that you didn't see—and who didn't see you. Even with winning or losing, there was no end to it. Always a midnight plane ride and skate, skate, skate the next night, and the next. Whether you are skating alone or in the game, whether the crowds were cheering or booing, you had to go on sore-muscled, winded or not; there wasn't anything else to do. So it was up and down and around and around for 78 games, and the endless warm-ups and practice sessions, and game after game without making an assist or a goal. These things were all part of the cost of doing what you had to do because it is your life. Skate, skate, skate . . . "

Ah, yes, skater, but what am *I* doing here? Hockey is neither my burden nor my joy. I must get off this ice before too many others appear to take up their endless round. I slip and slide apprehensively toward the gate, half-expecting another shower of ice shavings on my balding head. In their mercy I was spared, but I had to cross the traffic lanes on the rink's edge trusting in the increasing cloud of skaters not to collide. No more than a gentle, unnerving graze, please. I sat through the workout from the safety of the goal judge's booth—a cage sided with shatterproof glass.

"Well, what *are* you doing here?" asked Stan Mikita later, when I had hitched a ride in his car at the end of the training-camp workout.

"I'm writing a book on hockey in general and about the Chicago Black Hawks in particular," I explained. "As well as being a book for fans it is also to be for those people who have never been any closer to a hockey game than their television set. I'm going to try to explain to them what's going on out there on the ice as well as reporting my experiences firsthand as I learn about the game and hopefully get to know the team and players."

"You're not doing an exposé book, are you?" he asked suspiciously.

"No, I'm not," I answered honestly. "It's planned as I said. I'm not a professional sportswriter or a reporter, just a writer. A hockey layman."

"A *layman?*" quizzed the wise warrior, now in his fourteenth season as a Black Hawk. "Bobby Hull told me that you told him that you are an Episcopal bishop."

"So I am," I admitted. "A card-carrying bishop, and I also write books."

"Can you make the two go together?" Stan probed.

"I'm too dumb or overqualified to make a living out in the world in any other way, and I'm too old and too smart to be a hockey player." For an uncomfortable instant I felt that

I might be called for unsportsmanlike conduct, but Stan overlooked what could have been interpreted as a slur upon his vocation.

"I always thought that once a bishop, always a bishop."

"True," I said, "and I'm in the process of becoming a highly specialized one. With a little luck, I might emerge as the first S.O.B. in the National Hockey League."

"The *what?*" Stan demanded, looking at me as though I had high-sticked him.

"S.O.B.—Shepherd of the Black Hawks. How many professional sports teams have a bishop for a chaplain?"

"You know, it might not be a bad idea at that," Stan reflected. "We'll need everything going for us in order to win the Cup this season."

"You mean, like needing all the grace you can get?" I taunted.

"In professional sports you always do."

"Well, I'll try," I said, "but I don't have the influence with the Lord you may think. You see, Stan, I'm in sales, not management."

Confidentially, I suspected that he was relieved that the conversation soon took a turn in another direction as I began to give instructions on how to drive to my host's home. But the "interview" had been fun. Stan's natural cordiality had made me feel at ease.

My getting into the writing of a book on ice hockey had been strange. It began with a talk with my agent, as I handed him a manuscript. "What do you know about ice hockey?" he asked, out of the blue.

"Very little," I replied. "Like any boy growing up in the north-central part of the country I played a lot of shinny down back of the icehouse. Other than that my knowledge of the game is limited to having been to National Hockey League games now and then, down through the years. I also watch the sport on television and follow the fortunes of the teams, especially the Black Hawks. That's about the extent of it." I then asked him what he was driving at.

"An editor from Scribners was talking with my partner the other day about doing a book on hockey. Following a hunch, he asked Jim if he knew of anyone who would be interested in such a project. Jim mentioned it to me and it occurred to me that you might be the one."

"What *kind* of a book on hockey?" I asked cautiously, thinking that perhaps a search was on for a sports reporter.

"I think that what they have in mind is an in-depth book on hockey *by* a layman *for* laymen," he said. "The increasing popularity of the sport and the growing numbers of persons watching the game on television are creating a new audience that has never seen a game in person. If you are interested we can make an appointment with their editor, and then you can learn more about his idea."

A date was set for us to meet. What was desired, I learned, was a study in depth starting from outside the outer circle, from the armchair so to speak. It was evident immediately that the inquirer would have to start on the outside, immerse himself in the sport, and penetrate the bastions of big-time hockey to the very heart of the enterprise —the players themselves. It was understood that the only assistance that I would have would be a letter of introduction from the editor.

I prepared an outline of my plan of research. To my surprise, the idea and plan were accepted.

After the formality of signing the contract and receiving the initial advance—all purely a venture in faith on the part of publisher, editor, and author—I set forth in June, 1970, upon the assignment. I was far too committed to turn back and beginning to feel the beginning of anxiety as to whether this could be carried off. I was meditating upon how to go about the project as I slowly walked to the Penn Central station for my return home to break the news of my rashness to the family.

The adrenalin content of my bloodstream increased noticeably when I came in sight of Madison Square Garden which stands astride the railroad station. It loomed bigger and more formidable than it ever had before. It was only one of several fortresses that I would have to storm in order to write my story. Before I could learn what went on Inside Hockey, I had to find a way to be next to the ice and have access to the dressing rooms. A tall order, seeing as how I couldn't even buy my way. The Garden was already sold out for the season.

Such panicky thoughts were distressing, even on a sunny day in June. I lowered my head, supressed my anxiety, and took the train home to reflect upon what my curiosity had gotten me into this time.

2

Storming the Fortress

●

The first thing was to fly to Chicago and begin my assault on
the local citadel of hockey, the Chicago Stadium which contained the home and offices of the Black Hawks, including
that of Don Murphy, the director of publicity. I paced around
the outside of the building, trying to find a door that was
open. Externally the stadium seemed as deserted as an abandoned castle, but I *knew* that somebody must be inside, even
in July. I completed my tour of the walls, finding all doors
locked until I stood in front of the only untried one, numbered 3½—which seemed improbable. I pulled the door and

it opened. After a brief explanation and clearance of local customs, I followed a guard, who had quickly spotted me, into Mr. Murphy's office. The guard did not leave me until I had been delivered personally into the presence of the Director of Public Relations himself.

Murphy eyed me momentarily as though I had come all the way from the East to talk him into a season pass and free access to the Chicago Stadium to set up a private operation.

This man has undoubtedly listened to every pitch known to the sporting and entertainment world. Yet he was polite and reservedly cordial. The note from Scribners saved the day. I was given complete cooperation and granted access to the facilities and personnel. As with my editor, so it was with Murphy. It was made perfectly clear that I would have to make my own way, although every opportunity would be given to me for a toehold acquaintance with players and staff. The front office was willing to certify me and grant me entrée. The puck was passed back to me and by now I was truly beginning to enjoy the experience.

Don Murphy explained that it would be best this way in any case, and I agreed. "The boys have been burned before," he phrased it. Part of the sensitivity was no doubt due to the suspicion that I might be preparing to do an exposé of the personal lives of the Black Hawks on the order of Jim Bouton's *Ball Four* which was creating a cloudy stir in professional athletics.

Murphy recounted an incident of the past season when a sports columnist invited some of the players to lunch—at their own expense, it turned out. They drove to the restaurant and, parking the car in the lot, entered through a side door into the dining room. They had a couple of beers with their dinners, talked awhile, and then returned to the stadium for the afternoon workout. To their intense displeasure and righteous anger the report in the paper described sneaking in by the side entrance, getting boozed up, and returning to practice boisterously. Furthermore, the writer disclosed in his column some highly personal asides which had been made but which he had embellished and elaborated, distorting their original intent and meaning. "So that's what you're up against," concluded Don as he offered me another Coke from his office refrigerator.

After being informed of the opening date of the fall training camp, and receiving his invitation to attend, Don provided me with historical and promotional material on the Black Hawks. I was also provided with a desk where I could work at my own convenience when in the city of my numerous projected trips. Now I had nothing to do hockey-wise until September 14, the day when training camp would open at the Chicago Stadium. I took my leave with a slightly overdone expression of gratitude for his cooperation. The drowning man had been lifted into the lifeboat.

An empty and dimly lighted stadium is an enormous cavern. I laboriously climbed rank upon rank of the stairs to the top row and walked the circumference. Memories stood in the shadows like those of the six-day bicycle races of the twenties. I remembered the one and only football game ever played in this place, the National Democratic Nominating Convention of 1932, and the endless succession of sports contests of all kinds. The silent echoes of every event seemed to have seeped into the stone walls. This stirring of remembrance of things past became a personal liturgy of recall as in solo procession I measured off the tiers of waiting seats, descending row by row until I came to the arena floor and walked out where gladiators of past years stood their brave ground—athletes, politicians, entertainers—in a continuous line nearly fifty years long and still going.

On the flight home I realized that my talk with Murphy had been another point of commitment. My anxieties returned. The Black Hawk organization knew me now. I had made myself vulnerable, and now it was too late to turn back. I knew next to nothing of the road ahead. Could I gain the confidence and trust of the players? The old symptoms of panic started up again. There was no choice, only decisions—a sort of "Damn the torpedos, full speed ahead" act of will.

The hour had come to immerse myself in the sport completely. I read hockey rule books and manuals, biographies and autobiographies of the stars and superstars, books by coaches and books of hockey pictures. I induced the conversion experience which would make me into a hockey fan while still allowing me to retain an Olympian attitude of detachment so that I could write dispassionately. By the first of August I could think with authority about the sport. My mind was programmed with statistics on players, games, and ratings.

Yet, by the middle of August I began to lose this early confidence in my competency. The more I read, the less capable I felt to do the book. I took a hitch in my swim shorts and began doing exercises to strengthen my ankles for the season that lay ahead. My friends began to whisper behind my back, sadly shaking their heads as they noticed my increasing preoccupation and general social deterioration. This, in turn, fed the paranoid lurking within the shadows of my self. I brooded constantly. At last, I determined to go to New York.

Armed with my letter of authority which certified that Scribners actually trusted me to do the job, I sought out the director of public relations for the National Hockey League, Don Ruck. I was received by him with polite reserve and the offer of the cooperation of his office . From there I went next door to Madison Square Garden where the offices of the New York Rangers are and told my story and plans to John Halligan, the publicity director. Again, a cordial reception. So much exhibited trust and good will was beginning to unnerve me. By now I began to think that these P.R. lions had been forewarned and forearmed and were sweet-talking me to death. However, it turned out that they were honestly willing to help. Now, feeling much more secure, I took a trip down to the Spectrum, where the Philadelphia Flyers play, and explained my cause to Joe Kadlec. Sesame! Another door was opened. Again, it seemed too easy.

I thought, "Now comes the hard part."

3

In the Beginning...

●

The origins of hockey have been passed down to us in mythic form as have the stories of original sin. According to the ancient legends, both of them began in the Edenic state known as Persia. (Horseless hockey has been called "Persian Polo" for years.) Anthropologists make it clear that given a round object, such as a ball, man first had the impulse to throw it, secondly to kick it, and finally to hit it with a stick. Thus, hitting a round object while it was airborne, such as a baseball, must have been a later development of this fascinating business. It seems reasonable to suppose that hitting it along the ground came first, although today's hockey puck —that frozen, three-inch disk, that slipping and skidding piece of shrapnel—is a much more sophisticated missile.

There is evidence in ancient art that hockey has been around for a long time in one form or another. In the 1920's excavations in Athens, Greece, unearthed a bas-relief which showed a hockey face-off between opponents. This was dated at about 500 B.C., according to the archeologists. There is also some older evidence uncovered in Ur of the Chaldea, ancient Persia, which depicted two shepherds going at it with shepherd's crooks and a round stone. The French-Indian game of lacrosse also began with a stick and a ball. The "stick," however, then was a snowshoe.

There is also a clue found in the study of etymology, or word origins. The name, "hockey," apparently is derived from a French word, *hoquet,* which means "shepherd's crook." It is indeed a curious turn of evolution to discover that the shepherd's crook became not only the first hockey stick but also the symbol of office of a bishop of the Church. One can have no end of speculation on their common origin and the parallel development of both weapons. Bishops and goalies have a certain something in common—they are both defending something characterized by a net, whether it be to keep pucks out of or to get fish into. But one must remember that a shepherd's crook had a dual function: It was used to guide the flock on one hand and to drive off the wolves with the other. Its use as a hockey stick lies somewhere in between.

Roman soldiers adopted the game for their own. While one must admit that the Romans as a people were not particularly inventive or creative, they must be given credit for their remarkable ability to innovate and develop the other fellow's inventions and ideas. It seems likely that the Romans took the game westward and finally northward into what are now Europe and the British Isles.

Several centuries later hockey appears, phoenix-like, from the remains of the ashes of Roman military occupation. The Scottish version veered off into *shinty,* the ancestor of the game that so many of us played as boys on the frozen ponds, lakes, and rivers of America and Canada. *Shinty* means a "commotion or a brawl." No wonder the word has carried over into our day with the exchange of the *t* for another *n,* and is known as "shinny." However, in old Caledonia the shinty game ended with both teams gathered around a keg of whisky. I believe that a case might be made for the theory that this postgame recovery custom was the origin of modern postoperative intensive-care therapy.

The game was prohibited in Ireland in 1527 by the enactment of the Galway Statutes. "The horling of a litill balle with sticks and staves," was outlawed because of its savagery. Ironically, the lawmakers continued to allow the use of the shillelagh which seems to me to be a deadlier weapon. Yet, see what happened to the shillelagh. It degenerated into the fraternity paddle.

The Dutch were the first people to play hockey on ice. They called it *hut kolven* which has an ominous sound to me. In 1174 the game made its appearance in England marked by an unofficial and unscheduled brawl along the Thames River. There are two relics, or artifacts, still in existence which attest to the great age of the game in England. There is a stained-glass window at Gloucester dating from 1335 which depicts a hockey game of that period. There is also a pair of silver cruets which were recently discovered in an ancient church sacristy and which are engraved with crossed curved sticks and a ball.

The most interesting aspect of all, which testifies to the rigors and roughness of the game, was the action that King Edward III took to have the game banned. Hockey had become so popular that the reigning sport of archery went into decline. The Crown became concerned about the diminishing source of supply of skilled archers. A bow and arrow was considered a superior weapon to a shillelagh because you could knock off your opponent at a safer distance. Landowners were fined twenty pounds and sentenced to three years in jail upon conviction if they allowed their property to be used for "banned ball." From this edict came the name of the English version of hockey, called "bandy ball."

By filtering and sifting the myths and history of sports it becomes apparent that the birth of modern hockey took place in Canada. There are claims and persistent legends that it all began in Halifax, Nova Scotia, in the early 1800's. However, the earliest historical record of the games dates back to 1855 in Kingston, Ontario.

For over fifty years Her Royal Majesty's Canadian Rifles were stationed at the log fort which protected the lake harbor from "the noble savage" who wanted a larger piece of action in the fur business. In those days before modern warfare it was the custom for military detachments to hibernate or to go into winter quarters while the generals planned the spring campaigns.

For those of us who have read reports and stories of wintered forts, we know of the numbing boredom that set in as men waited out the winter. The plausible story comes down to us that their ennui became desperate. The commanding officer was going to have to act quickly in order to preserve either morale or sanity, for there was absolutely nothing to do between meals.

An anxious and enterprising officer had an idea. He instructed the blacksmith at the fort to make a couple dozen iron strips to be used for runners for skates. Holes were bored at either end of the runner to allow for thongs to be passed through so that the "skate" could be tied to army boots. I can picture vividly the entrance of the commanding officer into those barracks of boredom and his ordering the men out into the cold and down to the harbor on the edge of the parade around. Amid the grumbling and floundering a space was cleared of snow. The men were ordered to tie the iron runners onto their boots. They were supplied with lacrosse sticks with the nets removed. An old beat-up lacrosse ball was found to serve as a puck. Lo! The sport was born!

It must have been one of the funniest spectacles in the

annals of sport and the military when the troops found themselves on skates for the first time. Even the brass must have been uncertain as to how this maneuver would work out. The men obeyed orders and tried to skate. It has been reported that there were many endless delays in the game when the ball was hit out of bounds and disappeared in the snowbanks which bounded the rink area. I take it that these were automatic times-out in which the players sat down on the ice and wheezed breath back into their bodies. From all this, apparently evolved the present-day wood sideboards which delineate the out-of-bounds.

Kingston, Ontario, became known as the Bethlehem of ice hockey but the sport grew up in Montreal, Quebec, the Nazareth of the game.

Here is one of the reports of the new ice game that reached England: "These fellows have invented a game that is played on ice. They have fashioned knives which are fastened on their boots and they skate at each other in a menacing manner as they pursue a black rubber disc and propel it toward their opponent's wicket. There is a great noise and threatening as they advance toward the goal, brandishing their dangerous weapons at the enemy." It certainly wasn't cricket.

It was at McGill University that the game developed into the modern form. One of the first things that was done was to change the ball so that time would not be lost in retrieving it from snowbanks. This was easily accomplished by dividing a rubber ball into thirds and using the middle section. Lo! The puck!

Frederick Arthur, Lord Stanley of Preston, the Governor-General of Canada, started things going in 1893 by donating a silver trophy which is known as the Stanley Cup. He invested $48.67 of his personal funds in its creation. Since that time the Cup has had several bases added to it as the names of each annual winner have been engraved on it from that time down to the present. Presently it is between three and four feet high. This historically marks the emergence of professional hockey. The National Hockey League, formed about this time, took possession of it and to this day the Cup is the symbol of the League championship. During the playoffs for possession of this prize trophy the hockey world has pains two minutes apart awaiting the birth of the new champion every year.

Incidentally, United States sports fans who have grown up with baseball, basketball, and football became acquainted with the system of playoffs at the end of each sport to determine the championship in the respective sport. This has been viewed by fans as a revolutionary innovation. But Lord Stanley started it all in 1893. The big three of United States sports—baseball, basketball, and football—have borrowed it recently and have incorporated it into our way of doing things. How like the ancient Romans we Americans are. We also recognize a good thing when we see it.

4

The First Day

●

By the time that I had read and digested everything that I could find on the origin and development of hockey, I believed myself ready to go to training camp. As I expected, training camp turned out to be a benign and beneficial form of "concentration camp" in the original sense of the phrase. To use a less ugly phrase and a more felicitous explanation, this custom is ages old. It was only when the politicians and the military stole the principle, adapted and distorted it for their own use that "concentration camp" received its evil name.

In happier times it was known to our ancestors as a "retreat." From time immemorial, whenever a man or a group of men willingly separated themselves from the crowd the purpose was always to come to grips with a problem, personal or group, and come up with an answer by the end of the retreat, or time together. This was an ancient practice that remained pretty much as it had been until the time of the Russian scientist Pavlov. Best known for his experimentation with dogs, back at the beginning of this century, and conditioning their reflexes, Pavlov developed certain factors in what has become known as "brainwashing." These factors are unconsciously employed in training camps.

The first of these factors goes into operation with the setting up of a special "camp" which severs all ties with trainees' or rookies' families and friends. This makes it easier to break up the old behavior patterns so that the desired person may more easily be molded to the intended pattern. He is compelled to follow a rigid routine in an unfamiliar situation. A high fatigue level is maintained at a level just short of collapse. This is designed to keep him from being distracted by outside forces or gaining a perspective of what he is doing.

All of his time is to be used for learning totally new ways and adjusting to new and controlled situations. He must live in an atmosphere of uncertainty. He is ordered and encouraged to find his place in the order of things which he hopes will be acceptable to his superiors. A continuous state of tension is created and maintained in which the trainee or rookie becomes extremely anxious to please. He never knows what is acceptable or what he must do to receive approval—which is never given under any circumstances. He can only guess whether or not he is on the right track because he is never permitted to find out where he stands among those who count. He finds out only at the end of training camp when the "tail-cutting" takes place. It is a carrot-before-the-horse tactic which drives the rookie ever forward without any encouragement ever given which could possibly supply any hope that he might hear the words "Well done." Not only that, but should he be dropped from the squad and returned to a farm team he will never know what he did wrong or where he was lacking.

The camp, or retreat, is this prolonged period of probation under the most trying of circumstances. This period of training must be followed without question. It is indeed a period of probation although it goes by the name of "tryouts." The Biblical injunction "Many are called but few are chosen" is the recurring theme of training camps whether they be for professional sports or for the religious and monastic life.

Having conducted retreats and having been a fellow retreatant, too, I had an inkling of what was coming. I knew that I, too, as an outsider was in for a brainwash by the journalist camp. All the classic elements would be there. On September 14 the "retreat" began. I felt at home at once with the forces of psychological displacement that were already at work. I learned upon arriving that the Chicago Black Hawks are the only team in the League that conducts its training camp on home grounds. Still, the effects are felt. Even though the veterans whose homes are in the suburbs drive to and from the stadium daily, the rookies stay at a hotel in the Loop as guests of management. They are cut off even from the regulars when they return to their lonely cells in an impersonal hotel. Their contact with players and management is restricted to ice time. The rest of their day is spent in isolation, usually in the anxious and unhappy company of a colleague who doesn't know where he stands either.

Aside from my initial visit with Don Murphy in the early summer I had not been in the Chicago Stadium since the late forties. All of us can recall, usually with some twinge of pain, how changed the old neighborhood is. The hills have shrunk. The sliding hill isn't as steep as it used to be. When one is older one wonders where it ever came by the

21

name "Dead Man's Hill" or "Devil's Slide." The river isn't as wide as it used to be either. The icehouse which seemed as large as the Lee County Court House is a shabby, propped-up building leaning away from the prevailing wind and still resisting the inevitable.

But all that had changed on west Madison Street were the personnel of Skid Row. The replacements were playing the same roles, visiting on the sidewalk, lying in the alley or staring vacantly ahead into a tomorrow that would be a repetition of yesterday. The utter cheerlessness of west Madison Street had been accentuated by the razing of buildings here and there. Amid the carnage of fallen buildings stood an occasional structure still erect amid its vanquished colleagues. As far back as I can remember, the area has always been snaggletoothed in appearance and has had the fetid odor of decay and death in its remaining buildings and among its hapless denizens.

The stadium in its stony and craggy strength still remained the only symbol of stability and timelessness amid the graveyard rubble over which it towered, still strong and defiant of change. It had the patient appearance of a European cathedral which remembered that it was there first and would remain after everything else had crumbled into cindered parking lots cluttered with last week's newspapers, last night's programs, and yesterday's bottles emptied of sickly muscatel.

The cavernous nave was as large as ever. The huge pipe organ with its seven rows of keyboard and serried rows of stops looked down in haughty and regal red-gold splendor from its prominent throne and presided in toneless majesty awaiting the entrance of the nine-fingered master, Al Melgard. He designed the organ and has presided over it since its installation in 1929.

September 14, 1970, marked the first day of a journey that would take the Black Hawks on a journey of more than seven months of innumerable workouts and 78 games and through the Stanley Cup playoffs.

The First Day

In my naïve way I think that I expected to see the
rink filled with skaters making their way around fallen
figures, some writhing on the ice and others mercifully
inert and unconscious, bleeding profusely from assorted
wounds. But when I emerged from the catacombs and
corridors, which are laid out mazelike between the lobby
and the arena, and had my first look at the rink, I was
surprised. There was one skater slowly cruising around
the goal at the far end of the rink. However, there was a
crowd of skateless wonders down on the ice at the other
end of the rink. This whole area was cluttered with
television equipment in a state of partial assembly or collapse—I wasn't sure. Men were moving about this snake
pit of writhing cables, giving orders and directions that
nobody seemed to be paying any attention to. This crowd
seemed to be the same people who appear suddenly out
of nowhere at the scene of an automobile accident.

Television cameras were being set up near the players'
bench for the forthcoming interviews. The equipment for
photographing the still shots was already staged near the
other goal. The space for the action shots for publicity pur-
poses was set up midway down the ice in front of the penalty
boxes.

The solitary skater at the far end of the ice was being
joined by other skaters who appeared through the gate singly and intermittently. (The scene reminded me of the
check-in counter of an airport terminal when a celebrity is
about to arrive.) The photographers and interviewers would
beckon and call for the skaters one at a time to make their
way across the snake pit. The confusion was becoming
thrice confounded, what with the milling throng becoming
larger as the east gate kept grinding out more skaters onto
the ice. The scene became so familiar to me that I left chaos
to itself and made my way across the stadium to the gate
from which the skaters were emerging. I made my way
slowly against the stream of players coming up the stairs
from the locker room and I finally gained the holy of holies

itself—the dressing room and the training quarters of the Black Hawks.

There was very little conversation among the players in the process of suiting up. The medical examinations were being conducted and the shots administered in the training room. They were getting ready for a long trip. I felt that the subdued tone of voice and conversation was due to the crisis of training camp. Fully half the players would be dropped from the total squad by the end of the training-camp period. There was an air of understandable tension throughout the whole operation down here as well as upstairs on the ice. In spite of the absence of spoken orders or any awareness of direction, each person was intently engaged in *something* that made sense and gave direction.

In camp, one is never certain where the orders come from. Short, anonymous messages appear on the bulletin board and are never questioned. Fear and doubt are stimulated. The rookie has to wrestle alone and silently with anxiety and conflict. He begins to feel that his weaknesses are being sought out and that when they are discovered, they will be used in front of the group to make him foolish in the eyes of his colleagues. His dread and anxiety build up to this expected crisis. Should he fail to meet the unstated conditions of judgment he knows that he will soon be on the list of those who will be sent back to the minors.

Another important and often ignored factor is the absence of humor. It is not expressly forbidden, naturally, but under no circumstances is it ever employed. Any situation that would ordinarily provoke laughter is avoided. Should something ludicrous happen, mirth is personally controlled and suppressed. This rule goes at camp for superstar, veteran, management, and rookie. Tension and anxiety exude from the pores of everyone at the camp, even the press.

Living like this day after day produces mental, emotional, and spiritual exhaustion. A hysteria seems to be at the point of eruption all the time, but it never happens. It seems to me that this whole process of continued stress is designed to liquidate those who do not follow the implied pattern. The cynics and the humorous are the first to go. These two attitudes are strong defenses against the training-camp process. These persons are the least likely to be affected or controlled.

These factors may best be recalled in your own life when you moved into a strange town or neighborhood and made your first appearance at school and on the playground. You desire approval and acceptance. How are you going to achieve it? By conforming? or excelling? Probably a combination of both. But you sense that you are going to have to pass several criteria or tests. Any display of humor or joking is absolutely out. The only tactic that works in these situations is to adopt the "he-man" philosophy. That is, any show of sensitivity, warmth of feeling, or outward concern for another person is taken as a sign of weakness, a "feminine" trait. One soon learns on the street that a poker face is necessary to survival. This is regarded as meaning that the "poker face" is a person of great courage, superior strength and ability, and totally able to handle any and all crises. Compound this attitude and dynamic and you can begin to experience what the rookie is suffering. The training camp is his last stand, his crucial test. As on the playground of childhood, so it is here. If the test is failed one is consigned to having lesser lights as friends and playmates among the other castoffs of the playground elite.

In my role at training camp I reacted to the tensions as everyone else did. But I was required to meet a criterion that differed in kind but was of the same intensity. I did not have to go endure the rookie's ordeal. My bid was not for athletic collegiality. I was required to meet the unspecified demands and standards of the sportswriters, the journalistic fraternity. I was the suspected outsider, the unknown person, the possible fly in the ointment—until proven otherwise. The person who played the role of the playground leader of boyhood was the head of the Chicago *Tribune* Sports Department, Ted Damata. He knew who I was and I knew who he was but neither of us, following the law of the jungle, could go any further immediately. Protocol had to be followed unconsciously. I sensed that we were both a bit impatient with these tribal rules, but nevertheless they had to be obeyed. In the fullness of time this would be resolved. His rank and position as dean or chief would have been endangered by any show of interest or concern over the intruder.

Finally, my presence was outwardly admitted when the reporter who turned out to be the youngest and newest to have survived the ordeal approached me and began the discreet questioning. Now this all came out in the wash, of course, because they are men and they are human beings. It also works out for the rookie who is trying out for the team. But at the time it is a highly serious and precarious business. Remember, keep the stiff upper lip, your back to the wall, and never show a sign of weakness. Or, bang! You're dead!

I tried to stay out of the way. No one spoke to me nor I to them. As yet they were nonpersons. My lack of acquaintance with these men made it impossible for me to tell the difference between the rookie and the young veteran, the talented men, the stars, and the superstars. It seemed to me, as it probably did to many fans, that there should be an aura of charisma surrounding the great—or at least there ought to be some sign or tattoo mark or *something* that set them apart from the others. But I did not perceive any sign. The men who were suited up could be identified by their numbers and the brief biography that was given to the press for the occasion.

This opening day of training camp is hockey's Groundhog Day. Hockey players estivate. That is, they "hibernate" in the summertime. As far as the fans are concerned, I suppose that hockey players might be presumed to stay all summer in the basement clubrooms of the stadium waiting for the new season. They come above ground on opening day and then disappear for six weeks before they come forth finally, roaring into the the new season's schedule.

The First Day

I followed the last of the medically examined players up to the rink. By now the scene looked like a gigantic wedding rehearsal in a hugh church where everybody was a bridesmaid or a friend of the groom. The ceremony went its confused course in the better part of two hours at which time, like the finale of a ballet, everyone disappeared back into the ice at the east gate behind the goal. It left the impression this was all fantasy and hadn't really happened—like a Walt Disney production.

Directly back of the gate and the stairway to the training room was a sign marked "Aisle One." I went through the glass gate and entered a world strange and wondrous. I had already found my way through the underground labyrinth but following this other course I came out into a lobby.

There before me was an activated refreshment counter and a long table loaded down with all manner of food. There were strip steaks, beefburgers, and frankfurters. There were scrambled eggs to order and all kinds of cheeses, fruits, and jellos. There were canisters of broth. There were coffee, tea, milk, Coke, and Seven-Up. A holiday mood pervaded.

The reporters and writers, the radio and television men were the first to the table, having left their equipment out on the ice while the players had to take theirs off first. In due time the players showed up in stocking feet and a state of partial dress.

As the heroes of the world's fastest sport appeared for lunch they were an unglamorous lot. Like a benediction of bishops in a swimming pool, they all looked alike. Being out of distinctive uniform is a great leveler. These men were neither applauded, fawned upon, nor asked for their latest opinions on international diplomacy. Hockey wasn't even mentioned. Everyone was there to share the common meal. The players simply padded to the table and loaded their plates.

The decorum was similar to the Sophomore Hop at Platte City High School. The team sat at one end of the table. All the socially insecure media men huddled together in

27

silence at the far end, out of listening range and almost out of sight. Gradually, as the first plateloads were consumed, the men began wandering up and down picking seconds. The Prom became gradually mixed and the low buzz of conversation began.

I began to circulate about very slowly and casually, perceiving by their glances that I was an unknown factor in this setting. During my own search for a second dessert, I seated myself next to Bobby Hull, fate and decision apparently having started me out with a superstar.

Looking at me as though I were an enemy goaltender, he waited for me to make the first move, which I did before he had a chance to slap shot the conversational puck past me into the net of avoidance.

"Bobby," I began, extending the right hand of fellowship, "my name is Sterling. I'm contracted to do a book on hockey." He turned toward me slightly, took my hand, looked me up and down the way he judges stock on his Sasketchewan ranch. Then he smiled.

"What kind of a deal do you have with the head office?" he asked. The necessary and inevitable question.

"Strictly on my own," I explained. "I do not have any deal with management." After explaining about the book, I added "Bobby, I'm playing it straight with you men right from the start. I was the Episcopal Bishop of Montana for twelve years. That's the same brand as an Anglican where you come from in Canada."

"You mean that you quit a good job when you had it made?" he came back.

I smiled as I remembered a quotation from his own book, *Hockey Is My Game.* I reminded him that he was the founder of "TANS" (There Ain't No Security) and that I was only practicing what he had been preaching. I went on to tell him more than he probably wanted to know. "Being necessary and useful in a certain place comes to an end for bishops as well as for hockey players or other athletes. You have another career ahead of you on your ranch as well as other

business enterprises when your hockey days are over." I
could tell that we had gotten through to each other, but I
could see that it was going to take some time to get used to
the idea of a prelate preferentially associating with professional athletes.

By this time the lobby-converted-into-dining-hall had
gradually cleared of the diners. Several of the players disappeared into a room at the far end of the hallway so I decided
to snoop by and see what was going on. It was a room with
thirty cots placed in rows and covered with fresh green
sheets. The dim lighting reminded one of a cross between a
ward at the County Hospital and the Slumber Room at the
Creel Mortuary where the bodies "repose" preceding the
"viewing." Glancing at my watch I realized that there would
be a showing on the ice in about an hour.

I decided not to invade this sanctuary, recalling my earlier days as a pastor and all the anxiety that was generated
when I came into a hospital ward. The patients invariably
followed me with their eyes to learn who was about to receive last rites even though I dropped in as "Friendly Father." So I sauntered out on the ice and inspected the netted
goal. I didn't like the unyielding hardness of the iron bars
which supported the net. Skating into that would be as dire
as running into a goalpost while trying to catch a passed
football.

From the goaltender's eye-view in front of the net, the
rink stretched away to the western horizon. The mind's eye
saw a horde of skaters looming larger and larger before me
as they bore down yelling, waving hockey sticks, and advancing the puck toward me at a terrifying speed.

Suddenly the thin line between reality and fantasy was
broken. A monster red machine was bearing down upon me,
snorting and rumbling like a tank. It looked like a scavenger
truck. A very large young man was seated on top, keeping
the machine on the ice and waving at me to get out of the
way. I took it that he was Mr. Zamboni. At least that was the
name emblazoned on this juggernaut which seemed to be

actually eating up the ice. I vaulted over the boards and retreated to the box seats to watch the spectacle.

As I sat there, an unidentified member of the press corps came over and sat down beside me. He explained to me what this street sweeper was doing down there on the ice.

"The ice is prepared just before training season and it is left on through the whole season. This machine is used daily to maintain the ice in top condition. During the regular season games the rink is resurfaced during each rest period. The older the ice becomes, the harder it gets as the season advances. The first step is to spray a thin layer of hot water on the floor after the freezing equipment has been working for about twelve hours. This takes the frost off the floor and keeps lumps from forming. Then a layer of water about one-sixteenth of an inch thick is sprayed. After this a spray of whitening is applied which comes out of huge tanks which has mixed some stuff called Sunolith powder and other chemicals."

"I must go down into the basement and see all this," I said brightly.

"It's a plumber's nightmare," observed my guru. "There is also a machine there for deionizing the water. It freezes faster and stays harder longer."

"As with aging wines and spirits, it is better for the process," I said. [This fellow has the same problem that I do, I thought. He is telling me more than I need or want to know.]

"After the whitener has been applied, then a fine spray is used to seal it. Next, a quarter-inch of water is applied. The lines are then drawn and painted—"

"And that's when they put the emblems on center ice," I volunteered just to let him know that I knew what a rink looked like.

Undaunted, he was determined that I was going to get the whole course. "When this is done then water is sprayed again until an additional inch of ice has been added. This keeps the lines and markings from being scratched up by

30

skates. In about six weeks the skating surface is like marble, and the players begin to enjoy their skating."

"Enjoy?"

"Certainly! If you don't love to skate you'll never make a hockey player. These guys started on the ice before they had any memory function. It was love at first pratfall, so to speak." He could perceive that I had much to learn so he abandoned the "overteach" by suggesting that I note how hard the players have to work on this soft ice and how much easier the skating will go when the ice has aged.

It was some time later before I learned that this reporter who had administered first aid to me was Bob Verdi of the Chicago *Tribune* sports staff. He explained that this was only his second year on hockey. I could see that perhaps there was some hope for me. I was willing to accept the possibility that I was an object of pity at the moment and at the same time was being regarded as a colleague—rookie that I was.

Much of his relief, I suspect, the increasing noise in the stadium was making it impossible to talk. The carpenters and other workmen appeared to install the shatterproof-glass partitions around the rink. Repairs were being made to the boards, or sidewalls, bounding the ice. Strips of plywood were being nailed to the flooring where it met the boards so that spectators would not be dropping coins, catching heels, and losing personal effects under the stands. I presume that these precautions were taken in order to frustrate would-be suers of the corporation for insurance benefits. I'm catching on to the public.

The men had suited up and began appearing, one by one, on the refinished ice. The arena began to sound like a shooting gallery, what with the caroming of pucks off the boards. I referred to my folder on "Training Camp Information" and began to identify the players. I worked at this intensively for nearly an hour by which time the afternoon workout picked up tempo when Coach Billy Reay slowly and quietly skated to center ice. The bombardment stopped. The

31

men, without a word or signal that I could discern, began skating slowly round and round the rink. The coach blew his whistle. Everybody stopped on the spot and reversed direction. In a moment there was another blast, and the squad broke into a sprint as though the building was on fire and everybody was making for the exits. They roared by the coach at full speed, decelerated on the backstretch, and broke into a full sprint again when they passed Billy's reviewing stand.

After a short breather the squad was divided in half. Each group lined up on a blue line facing the goal 60 feet distant as the goalie slowly skated toward the net, ready for the assault that he knew was coming. I admired the resignation in his manner as he skated to his doom. Each man took a turn at bringing the puck down the ice and trying to put it in the net. There was a continuous heavy stream of men and pucks coming at this poor man, and soon the goal became well filled with pucks. Everything stopped while the goalie raked them out and dropped some more out of the folds of his jersey. They were taken back to the blue line and the whole business started again, except that a relief goalie replaced the battered incumbent. This drill must have seemed endless to him. The marauders and disturbers of his peace stood around the blue line, chatting and waiting for their turn with a puck.

Nor was this the end of the workout. Now three men, a center and two wings, would pass the puck between them at high speed and make a hostile call at the goalie's home, only to skate away grinning when he slammed the door on them. After this had gone on long enough to fill the net with pucks again, the goalie was given a little help as the defensemen joined in the fray to practice breaking up the plays.

The total workout lasted about an hour and a half, concluding with the usual wind sprints and the fast starts and stops. A feeble tweet of the whistle signaled the end of the session. By this time the perspiring players could have heard an emphysemic wheeze in a foundry. They disappeared except for five or six who stayed behind to practice shots. I ventured down on the ice and cautiously slid my way to a safe place behind the goal net crouching down in order to experience, at least to a degree, how a goalie felt when a puck came at him.

Those fine fellows out there practicing shots cooperated beautifully and apparently got a kick out of watching me reflexing here and there. The shots came so fast and furiously that I was stepping into one puck as I avoided another. Even though I was on the safe side of the net, nature kept preserving me through my involuntary recoils. When a puck would come sailing at me at about 100 miles per hour (that's the speed at which they have been measured), it appeared to be about the thickness of a calling card and having the penetrating ability of a laser beam.

Dennis Hull, Bobby's brother, called out, "Go up and sit in the goal judge's box." At first I thought that he was politely telling me to get the hell off the ice, but he wasn't. The goal judge's box is a large glassed-in booth with a glass top a little larger than a telephone booth and is situated right behind the goal. He can see everything that's going on in the flailing mayhem in front of the net when there is a loose puck. He determines when a score has been made, pressing a button which flashes on the fateful red light which goalies abhor. I felt unscolded and important as I entered the booth and fastened the door. No sooner had I perched myself on the stool and gazed about in isolated splendor than the barrage began. Rubber shrapnel crashed onto my booth. These fellows 60 feet out on the blue line were lifting their shots *over* the net and goal and aiming them directly at me in my turret. The noise was louder than a hailstorm on a henhouse roof. Involuntarily I ducked from the sound and covered my ears, which seemed very funny to the shooters out there on the ice. There was no escape. I couldn't leave until they ran out of pucks. I spent a day there during the next five minutes. Finally they ran out of ammunition, interest, and energy at the same time and began skating in characteristic slow lazy strokes around the rink. I climbed out of my glass cage and stood in the front row of seats watching them go around as I absently recovered myself. I wasn't watching too closely, apparently, for I didn't see Pat Stapleton skating around on my left. At the instant he went by me he rapped the protective glass a mighty swat right alongside my nose. I didn't know I had any reflexes left after my ordeal in the goal judge's booth, but there was one big jump left in me. That made one big laugh for Stapleton and his friends—by now on the opposite side of the rink. I took this as a hopeful sign of beginning acceptance of having me around.

The present seemed as good a time as any for me to introduce myself to Billy Reay. I decided to trap him in his office lair and confess the reasons for my presence (as if he didn't know already). I experienced some funny feelings en route to the court as I hastily organized a plan to explain my pure motives and indubitable naiveté. Previously, during the workout upstairs on the ice, I was impressed by his control of the situation. Every order was complied with instantly upon the blow of his whistle. No questioning. No doubt about what he meant. No discussion, grumbling, or arguments. Of course I realize that every leader of men is expected to be able to command and get away with it. But this was total. He blew his whistle. He motioned. He spoke softly and evenly. He was a great ringmaster. The players, veterans and rookies alike, went through the repertoire workout without hesitation or question.

There is a parallel here between coach and players that is striking in its similarity to a lion tamer. I was immediately reminded, naturally, of Daniel in the lion's den. Daniel's secret of control was his ability to avoid crossing the critical distance line. The lions all knew where it was. Daniel had to guess. I recalled the lion tamer in the circus. His whip, chair, and pistol were all trappings. They were simply props to which the lions didn't pay the slightest attention. These things were for the customer's delight.

What the lion tamer *must* know intuitively is where the

lion thinks the critical distance line is at any given time, for this must not be crossed. The tamer and the lion both understand that they have interactive responsibilities toward each other if they are both going to eat regularly. Certain things are expected to be accomplished. But this doesn't make the tamer into a lion or vice versa. They have their separate worlds and a place of meeting, critical distance line and all.

I began to feel an affinity for Reay and I had not yet met him. It was easy for me to identify with both coach and players in terms of my own experience. I had had an eighteen-year period as a pastor. I worked under a coach. He is called a bishop. I suppose that I could have been termed an ecclesiastical hockey player. I was always moving fast, always going somewhere, and always on the thin ice to which I have alluded. Sooner or later I met up with the goalie, the bishop's secretary. Sometimes I could get past her but my average was low. Later on in my ministry I learned how to get around her but by that time I had slowed down. Then, by a strange turn of events I became the bishop.

Coaches, having been hockey players themselves at one time, even as bishops were once pastors, should be able to understand any affinity or sense of collegiality that we might have between each other. This change of role through the years also helps me to understand the coach and his reponsibilities. In hockey language I, as a bishop, was always looking for a new center, a left wing, or a right wing, or a first-class defenseman who could put the diocese in contention for the Holy Grail. I never looked for a goalie because I already had a good secretary and in an emergency I would do my own goaltending.

Reay's office was adjacent to the locker room, the treatment room, and the equipment cave. I had not long entered these sacred halls before I sensed that the coach's office either had an invisible moat around it, an electric fence, or that it was quarantined. Everyone passed around it.

"He has a job very much like a bishop," I reflected,

remembering the years that I had spent on Mount Olympus, aloof, friendless, and isolated, being addressed only when someone had some advice to offer me "for my own good, of course." Even my goalie secretary regarded each crisis as being either too trivial to bother me with or so important that it would upset me. So I ruled in lonely and uninformed splendor.

I peeked around the corner into Billy's office before knocking on the open door. Except for his baseball hat and sweat shirt he could have been a bishop. All of the above agenda had been buzzing around in my head so loudly that I approached his eminent domain in the same manner that I had used as a young pastor when I had been summoned before the episcopal presence on what was known as the "purple carpet." It was unnecessary. As I entered his office his manner was like that of an archbishop having an appointment with a stranger whom he suspects might be trying to sell him a sliver of wood from the True Cross.

His office was no larger than 12′ by 12′, in my estimate, having a desk and an experienced swivel chair in it as well as six armless straight chairs against two walls facing that desk. The walls were covered with both portrait and action-shot pictures of hockey players of past years, all of whom, I think, were teammates and colleagues of Billy Reay in his playing days in the League. There were also prominent pictures of the scene following the Black Hawks' capture of the Western Division the previous year when they zoomed from last place to first. The desktop was the same as any manager's who works without a secretary—a foot deep in paper, giving the impression that he alone knew where everything was.

Billy is a small man, even by hockey standards. During his eight years as center with Montreal he never weighed more than 155 pounds. He was in excellent physical shape, facially unscarred except for the bent nose which seems to be the identifying mark of most athletes and all hockey players. He struck me immediately as being not only highly intelligent but savvy.

Introducing myself, I explained my unexplainable presence in this sanctuary. I was armed with my letter from my editor, which he read quickly and dropped into the center drawer of his desk. Then he waited, as athletes do in the arena, for the opponent to give a slightest of hints as to which way he was going. I perceived a certain thawing in his manner, albeit I also detected that he was not about to be faked out of any play. Apparently he received at face value my remark that I was not going to busybody around the place, collecting questionable anecdotes about everybody in order to fill the pages of a book.

He welcomed me in his aloof, tense, and self-conscious way. I was made to feel that I could come and go through his domain without question of apprehension to the same degree only as could other members of the press.

As I walked out of his cubicle of an office, I noticed a blackboard on the wall in the entryway to the dressing room. The only thing on it was a laconic announcement:

SCRIMMAGE TUESDAY
10:00 A.M.

5

Laws and Order

●

Hockey is an exciting and fascinating combination of speed, courage, and *order.* That last may surprise you but it's true. A rink is about 200 feet long and 85 feet wide. It is paved with the world's hardest ice. Compared to rink ice, glacier ice seems as soft as slush. Besides being vertically thin, hockey ice is thin in a symbolic sense, too. One never knows when there is going to be a collision and a traffic jam. Sometimes that's even planned, like in a stock-car race.

The rink is segmented by three lines: two blue and one red. The blue lines are 60 feet in front of each net. The red line divides the rink in half. The lines are designed to keep certain players out of certain zones under certain conditions under penalty of trespass. The areas between the blue lines and the "cages," or goals, are known as defensive zones. The space between the blue lines bisected by the red line is the neutral zone. Being found in the wrong zone is as embarrassing as a man's finding himself in a ladies' room. He can approach but he mustn't enter. Doing so is illegal and creates unnecessary excitement.

Here is where the problems begin. You can't pass beyond the red line. A puck carrier can skate the puck out and take it as far as he wants to—at his own physical risk. As soon as the puck is beyond the first blue line, it can be passed up to the next blue line. Simplified, the rule is that you can't pass the puck across two lines. This compares, in a certain sense, to basketball in which the ball must be advanced from beneath the opponent's basket to mid-court in ten seconds. From mid-court you have twenty-four seconds in which to move the ball down for a shot. In these two games there are restrictions on advancement although they operate in different ways.

The puck must always precede all attacking players over the red line and over the defending team's blue line. Any violation of this rule is called an "offside." This means a "face-off" at the nearest face-off circle, or marking for that purpose on the ice. In a face-off the referee drops the puck between two facing players. The center circle, like that in basketball, is used for the start of each period of play.

Sometimes you'll see a player skating down-ice and suddenly pull up as he approaches a line. The reason is that if he crosses that line ahead of the puck, he's offside. This rule keeps him from skating on ahead and cruising around the opponent's net while waiting for a buddy to send the puck down to him for an easy shot with no one in his way but a fierce and nervous goalie.

If a team gets down the ice into the last zone and then loses the puck to the other team, the first thing the other team will try to do is to clear the zone and move down the ice toward the other goal. If they do, then the first team must clear the zone, too. Sometimes it reminds me of a herd of cars trying to get the jump on a changing traffic light. The goalie can stay back, of course. He remains behind to gather up strength and nerve for the next assault.

Speaking of the goal, that cage or net is 4 feet high and 6 feet wide. It is reported to look like crack in a bank vault door to an attacker. To a goalie it looks as big as the door to a cathedral. Notice that in front of the net there is a small rectangular area marked off in red. This is the goalie's crease. It is out of bounds for the attacking forwards. Should a puck go into the net when a member of the offense is inside getting chummy with the goalie, then the goal is not allowed and the offending player is in grave danger of either being eaten alive by the goalie or beaten senseless. There is an exception to this: In case an attacker is shoved or pushed into the maw by a defenseman, he can get out alive and without penalty.

We aren't through yet. There is still another red line to be explained: large half circles at center ice and along the sideboard on one side. They are the referee's crease. It reminds me of a pulpit without steps or railing. When an argument starts on the ice the referee makes a judgment call and then skates away from the scene of the crime and goes into his crease. Once he gets inside, none of the players can talk to him. Just like the fellow in the pulpit that you can't talk back to until after the service. The area inside that crease is a sort of coward's castle. If a player crosses that line he keeps right on going to the dressing room, possibly right on out to the street, in certain undefined circumstances.

By the way, of the three officials on the ice, only one is the referee and only he can call fouls and administer penalties. He runs the game. The other two are linesmen who may advise the referee about the rules but who are officially there to call offsides and "icing."

"Icing the puck" means shooting the puck the length of

the ice, over and beyond the opposing goal in order to get it away from your net and break up an opponent's attack. When this happens the puck is returned to your end of the ice for a face-off, which gives the other team a chance to gain control. Icing the puck gets it out of your hair temporarily and gives your team a breather. These occasions are sometimes used to advantage by allowing time for substituting. That's one way of getting a fresh offensive team on the ice when there is no provision for a time-out. It's a strategic move to take off the pressure.

When a team may be shorthanded because there are teammates in the penalty box then it's all right to ice the puck. You need every break you can get when you're shorthanded because you know that the opposition is going to use a power play on you.

A power play occurs when a team has an advantage in manpower because some of their opponents are paying for sins by sitting in the penalty box. (Actually, it is the remaining team that pays for the sinner's transgressions.) The shorthanded team is interested in one thing only and that is killing time efficiently. This is called killing the penalty or eating up the ice until their teammates have been absolved and can skate a free men once again and join in the fray.

To "kill" a penalty, what is left of the team uses what is called a box defense. Four men (if they have that many exclusive of the goalie) form a square in the defensive end of the rink. Each man is expected to cover a specific zone. There is no choice but to prevent a score until their penalized colleagues are allowed back on the ice. The four boxmen are there to recapture the puck and ice it back to the other end of the rink so that the offensive team has to reorganize and start another play. It's a dangerous business, playing keep-away in hockey, just as much as defensive ball-control in basketball is only for the supercompetent.

Although the next maneuver may sound like a move in chess it is considerably more violent and noisy. It's called a forecheck. This means getting in your opponent's way, at least by the time that he reaches center ice, or the neutral zone. Backchecking means falling back after your attack in order to defend against the other team and being as big a nuisance to their game as possible without being ordered to the penalty box, the locker room, or chased down an aisle.

Watch for the fellow who doesn't try to backcheck. He is the one who is goal-hungry. He cruises around out there in the neutral zone, waiting for the spark from heaven to fall in the form of a free puck. The spark doesn't fall every day, especially in National Hockey League competition. He'd be helping his team considerably more by roaring into his zone and frustrating an attacker.

There is a demonstrable theory about the similarity between a watchdog and a goalie. The watchdog, as every burglar knows, is very ferocious and brave when he is inside his own crease. All canines know this well, too. An invader ambles into his front yard—his crease, so to speak. The watchdog—the home team—takes off after him. His courage decreases in direct proportion to his distance from his yard. Reversely, the chased picks up courage as he comes closer to his own crease. In turn he becomes the chaser. Of course, this is what the red line is all about. It is hockey's version of the critical distance line that all creatures, including man, observe with each other. (There are certain lines one does *not* cross, etc.)

Goalies are fine fellows when you meet them at center ice. They are fine fellows off the rink ice, too. But don't make the mistake of thinking that this cordiality is going to apply when you skate by the front of his cave. He'll slice you up if you come in close.

To the approaching offense player, the goalie wearing his portable fort and breastplate of raw guts looks like a man-eating giant. He seems to grin in a fiendish glee, showing all forty-two teeth in rows like a shark's. You know that he eats raw hockey pucks, salted or not. The goalie frightens me even when he isn't wearing his protective face mask. It is to the goalie's advantage to cultivate this kind of image.

If he is respected as a man-eater this may produce a split-second reluctance to skate too close to the net, thus reducing chances to score.

Back in the old days the goalie had a lot of free time on his hands. He had the leisure to function as the team philosopher and keep contact with his teammates on one of the infrequent calls of the opposition in charge of offense. Aside from the occasional forays of the opposition and collecting stray pucks in the teeth, the goalie led a contemplative life. Now all that has changed. There are different rules, now. His end of the rink has become a shooting range and he is always in the line of fire.

In spite of his armor and skill, he has become the most vulnerable man on the ice. The new way could easily make a paranoid of him. Like a little old lady trying to cross the freeway cloverleaf on foot during the rush hour, the goalie darts back and forth. Traffic is always heavy. There are screen plays which are designed to keep him from seeing what's going on. There are power plays and deflects—plus a 78-game schedule. Suddenly goalies have become victims of more injuries, emotional upsets, and tortured minds than the rest of the team put together. Lightning is always striking, even in the same place twice or more often.

Since the rules changes which have sped up the game, the goalie has come up with a kind of stress that is new in competitive athletics. In a way his lot compares to that of a baseball catcher, except that the latter gets a change of duty by taking a turn at bat and chasing pop flies. He doesn't squat there all through the game stopping hot rivets. The goalie does, and there isn't any way that he can get even. He's too busy trying to keep from having the puck jammed down his throat. He has no outlet for his feelings. A defenseman can ease his pressures by popping an opponent just for the sake of relief. The wing can skate furiously up and down the ice leaving a trail of steam as he works off his overproduction of adrenalin induced by a previous crisis. What about the goalie?

He can't do a thing but wait for the next onslaught, a power play perhaps, all the while muttering a few curses to himself, composing a few maledictions, and brace himself to absorb the next flying puck—if he can see it first. It isn't long before he takes every attack toward the goal as a personal affront. As you watch the game you can see how easy it must be for a goalie to believe that every launched offensive is directed personally at him.

A center, a wing, or a defenseman is expected to make a mistake and to lose the puck sometimes. If a goalie does so, it costs the team a goal. It is easily the toughest job in sports.

Jacques Plante, the veteran goalie, observes, "Only a goalie can appreciate what a goalie goes through." Having watched from the safety of the goal judge's booth, I can now understand that the hazards are unbelievable. The shot is a screaming blur. If you blink an eye it is gone. Jacques considers himself lucky if a 100-mile-an-hour shot hits him, for the chances are 50-50 that he won't see it coming. All he must do is to step into the shot. That's what he is supposed to do. It is a thankless, unglorious, nerve-shattering job.

Tony Esposito complains that it's the slap shot that makes the difference. "Today everybody has one—or thinks he does, and they're the most dangerous. The curve can drive a goalie crazy—or kill him. It makes the puck rise, drop sail off—a knuckle ball at 100 mph. If a man ever gets control of the curved stick the goalies would be better off blowing their brains out before they get knocked out. This way it's a slow death at best."

And that's what Masked Icemen have to say about The Game and their jobs.

Another major difference between other team sports and ice hockey is the absence of set plays. In football every play starts from the scrimmage line. Time is allowed for the players to pick themselves up, come to the line of scrimmage after a huddle, and set up another play. In basketball one can watch a set play develop. In hockey there are plays, too, but the movement is so fast that it takes careful watching practice to follow them. Only in hockey does a play begin at twenty-five miles an hour and move through heavy traffic at that speed. Nor are there huddled plans before or after-wards.

Let's pretend that you have made the last payment on your car. You drive onto the expressway, driving it home in triumph. This is like the start of a hockey play—Possession. All that you have to do is get the prize home. (Hockey players *never* skate with their head down.) All the time that you are driving your car you are living in an imminent state of colli-sion. What happens to you when somebody sideswipes you, messes up your control, and slams you against the guide rail? If you're still conscious and can get out of the car, you are in a fighting condition and ready to rack up that bum. So, too, in hockey.

You may emerge from your car raging and waving the stick shift in your hand, intent upon murder. That is the motorist's version of the hockey stick—that and the steering shaft. Some bum broke up your play, and he's going to pay for it. You may be angry enough to take a swing at him. Along comes the highway patrol. What happens? You are escorted to the penalty box. The only difference is that you can use a phone and call your wife, lawyer, and insurance man. The hockey player sits it out in the penalty box without benefit of counsel. No bail. He serves time.

Can you begin to see how easy it is for us Armchair Alberts to identify with the hockey players?

That's you down there on that ice. That puck is the pay-check or the new car, that raise or promotion. Here comes some bastard trying to take it away and decapitate you at the same time.

(Hockey players *never* skate with their head down.) Witness your alter ego down on the ice. He overcomes every obstacle. He skates through traffic jams and all roadblocks. He gets to the door—the goal. The entrance is blocked. Two of his confederates skate into sight but they are too late. The goalie alone remains. Your identity tries to "deke" him out

45

of position. He is dared to skate away from the door. Then with a sudden turn and a flick of the stick, the prize is home, in the net.

"I could do that, too, if things had only been different in my life. I know I could—if only . . ."

6

What Every New Fan Should Know

●

Training camp wasn't turning out as I had envisioned it during my more feverish moments of the last summer. The glamour and excitement went out of it before camp began because there were no plans whatsoever for the squad to be flown to northern Canada for a thirty-day quarantine and isolation. Nor was there such a thing as a curfew. The "camp" was right there in the Chicago Stadium only a mile and a half from the Loop downtown business section. The squad showed up one and two at a time from their homes in the city and suburbs. The rookies who had been invited to come to the "camp" and try out were stationed at a down-town hotel and came out every day by bus. The "training table," loaded down as it was with high-quality protein food in abundance, provided the noon meal only. As soon as the workout period was finished, everybody showered and dressed and presumably went home.

Upon reflection, though, one should remember that these men were adults fighting for their jobs. This was serious business. They didn't need chaperones or truant officers. The camp provided an opportunity for them to qualify as a team member. Each man's basic need and desire was to excel, to merit selection, and end up among the chosen remnant—the final eighteen allowable skaters out of the forty present who were aspiring to this distinction.

Coming to a training camp under these conditions was a sober and sometimes desperate business. One anonymous aspirant, a stranger sitting alone and somewhat forlorn at the emptied training table, confided that he was twenty-nine years old this year and that if he didn't make the team this time, he was washed up. He told me that he had played ten years of minor league hockey, so it was now or never for him. He explained that there were eight others competing with him for the position, remarking wryly that all of them were only twenty or twenty-one years old. As it turned out later he not only stayed on but saw a lot of ice action.

In watching the skaters go around and around the rink in a big circle and getting the feel of the ice after a summer's layoff, I began to notice the difference between the rookie and the veteran. The differences in age and number of battle scars were not the determining factors in which was which. It was the look of controlled anxiety that crept onto the faces of the newcomers that set them apart. Definitely they were not at ease nor practiced at it as compared to the men who had played more than one season in the National Hockey League.

The rookie had a marked eagerness and desire to be watched and looked at. He skated harder in the warm-up.

He was generous with his energy output. He was all-out for being noticed and, he hoped, recognized as a standout among the strangers. I could see that it was absolutely essential to him to score points at training camp if he was to have even the slimmest of chances to be chosen to enter the ranks of the most high—the playing members of the NHL.

It is not a farfetched comparison to draw a parallel between the rookie contenders and the young Indian braves out on their first big-game hunt with the tribal braves who had already established themselves. In both cases it was critically necessary that they excel the first time out on the hunt or they could be relegated to the ranks of the stay-at-homes to do the menial tasks within the tribal traditions. They must kill their first buffalo. In their eagerness to gain rank and status the young braves frequently gave away the marauding party's strategy and location because of their anxiety to be the first to the kill, thus exposing everyone to danger. An ancient medicineman, Noah Bear Robe, had survived 93 Dakota winters. He explained to me that until a brave could return to camp with a trophy of the hunt it was almost impossible for him to have any status. The women either rejected or ignored him. He was nobody—the low man on the totem pole. The older and seasoned warriors and hunters were established and proven. They did not have to win their position in the tribe but simply to maintain it. I began to see this pattern emerge here at training camp.

The veteran's attitude toward a rookie is similar to an older brother's noticing that his younger brother is growing up. He may help him if he is asked with proper deference to his rank and established superior ability and experience. He is not likely to go out of his way in offering any assistance. It is unthinkable that any veteran would tout to the coach what promise he thought a certain rookie might have. Basically they are competitors.

One could sense the mounting tension as the men skated slowly around the rink, warming up for the scrimmage and with the day of judgment close at hand. When the scrimmage began the competition of the rookies for the coach's attention became intense. There was also the need to impress the veterans as well as their rookie colleagues.

Billy Reay was always the sole referee during the scrimmages. From the sidelines one could never detect whether or not he said anything to the players while lining up for a face-off. My early impressions of coaches, gained through high school experience plus years of being interested in sports, made me believe that they were bullies, ever driving the men on by insult, epithet, and ridicule. As far as I was ever able to determine, Billy never lost his cool when working with the men on the ice. He was the first quiet coach I had ever known. I could see that he had a controlled fire and that if he ever opened up on anyone it would have to be behind the closed doors of the dressing room where even angels would fear to tread. A sort of the seal of the confessional was on whatever was said by the coach, or anyone else as far as I was ever able to find out.

The squad was divided at the beginning of scrimmage into five teams which were frequently alternated. There was very little conversation between the men on the bench awaiting their turn to go out and give their all. I began to notice that the regulars skated just well enough and played just hard enough to let the rookies know that they still had things to learn. The regulars had a distinct advantage in that they knew their teammates' playing styles and knew about where they would be on the ice at any given time. Each improvement or correction by a rookie was met by a more sophisticated tactic by the veteran. If your psychological need is for approval by your betters, then don't go to training camp.

In order to get as close to the action as possible during the scrimmages and still not run the risk of decapitation from a flying puck delivered by a zealous rookie, I took a seat in the penalty box. This arrangement is directly across the ice from the player's bench and consists of two "cells" walled all around with a material called "herculite," a shatterproof glass. The timekeeper and penalty judge are seated between the penalty boxes for each team. When the scrimmage began I was surprised to notice that the goaltenders did not sit on the player's bench when they were off ice but skated over to the penalty boxes and conducted their own caucuses there. I soon learned that they are a species apart from their colleagues who play either offense, center, or defense. They have a special set of problems that go with their way of life that naturally separate them from the rest of the team.

At the time there were six goaltenders competing for two jobs. According to the National Hockey League rules, Tony Esposito explained, a team may carry and suit up only two goalies. Both he and Gerry Desjardins were sophomores or second-year men with the Black Hawks last year. They were certain to retain their jobs in the coming year. Nevertheless, the rookie goalies were giving out with everything they had. I was surprised, though, to see these two "lettermen" patiently and generously explaining the fine points of goaltending to their would-be rivals. "The least I can do is help a goalie survive whenever he's sent down," explained Gerry Desjardins. Their highly specialized skills place them apart as a professional group. Trying out for a goalie position on the Black Hawks this year seemed to be a hopeless cause—except for what one might learn from such men.

Tony Esposito had been rated the best goalie in the National Hockey League for the 1969–70 season. He received the Vezina Trophy, which is awared to the goalkeeper having played a minimum of twenty-five games for the team having the fewest number of goals scored against them. He had also been named rookie of the year, having achieved a record of fifteen scoreless games. As if that were not enough for a rookie to contend against there was also Gerry Desjardins who is far from an ordinary backup goalie and relief man. He can hold his own, even against Tony. It is no small wonder that the rookies listen to these men.

Tony commented to me, in answer to a question about

the rookies from Yugoslavia who had come over to try and break into NHL hockey. "These boys are very good," he said, "but they are seeing stuff on this ice in our game that they have never seen over there. They aren't ready yet for the Canadian-American style hockey in this League."

Another strong impression made during this first all-out scrimmage was the size of the players. Being used to watching American football and basketball players, I suppose that I took it for granted that National Hockey League players would also be the same size as these superbly coordinated giants of American sports. The tallest of them were 6'2"— Bill White and Eric Nesterenko. Each of them weighed a little under 200 pounds. As athletes go, that isn't very big or hefty. Bobby Hull, superstar, is 5'10" and weighs about 195. Most of the men were around 5'7" to 5'10" and weighed between 165 and 185 pounds. That's not big by American sports standards. But I was amazed at their speed, change of pace and direction, and had an immediate and profound admiration for their grace and coordination. To this day I never tire of watching them, particularly Nesterenko, who swoops, dips, and curves in graceful arcs and always seems to be soaring around waiting for the puck to come squirting out of the crowd of "diggers." When I asked him how he usually managed to be there at the split moment when he was needed, Eric smiled and in his slow reticent manner said, "When you have skated as many years as I have you sorta know where it's coming." Eric is thirty-seven and was playing National League Hockey when Joe Namath was in grade school.

I remarked to Bobby Hull about Eric. "You know, Bobby, Eric says that he likes to skate, even after all these years."

"He's nuts, like the rest of us," Bobby retorted. "He's played hockey so long, he doesn't know any better any more."

When the scrimmage session had been completed I drifted down to the dressing room and introduced myself to "Skip" Thayer, the trainer and body-repair man. His sanctuary was gleaming white; it contained two examining and treatment tables and an assortment of mysterious jars of ointments and salves as well as a whirlpool bath and a refrigerator. The latter contained not only medicines necessarily kept under refrigeration but several cans of soft drinks and a couple dozen pucks which are chilled before use. It reduces their erratic motion and behavior on ice. Simple. Practical.

Two of the players were stretched out on the treatment tables having muscle bruise problems administered to. Others sauntered in and out on minor errands for adhesive tape and other things. Bobby Hull came into the room as the telephone rang.

"City morgue," he announced like a character out of a murder movie on a television rerun. He motioned Thayer to the phone. A reasonable degree of respectful quiet was observed. Doug Jarrett was lying on one of the tables awaiting Thayer's return from the phone. He was holding a jar of Atomic Balm that Skip had handed to him. Those in the room were quiet not only because Thayer was on the phone but because there was a stranger in the room whom they were not sure of, so I thought, and rightly. I went over to Doug and asked him a stupid question as to whether or not the goo was hot.

"Put your finger in it and see," he said as he offered me the jar.

I stuck my forefinger tentatively into the jar and got some of the goo on the tip. "It doesn't seem to be so hot," I remarked. "What does the stuff do? Does it work inside?"

"Rub your finger and your thumb together," Doug instructed me.

I did as he said. Immediately the heat started up my hand to my wrist and up my arm to the elbow. The arm felt like a torch and it became red. No one moved a facial muscle but waited and watched me for signs of collapse. It flashed through my mind that the law of any jungle was operating again and that the first person to show any sign of breaking would be excommunicated. There was nothing for me to do but stand and be consumed in front of them. I walked slowly over to the sink and turned on the cold-water tap in order to put the fire out. No relief.

"When does my hand break out in flames?" I asked as calmly as I could, feeling my body temperature soaring up to at least 109 degrees.

"What are you complaining about?" asked Jarrett. "You should have a smear of that on your behind."

"I would outsprint everybody on the squad," I answered. "I wouldn't even make the curve at the end of the ice. By then I'd be airborne. What's in that stuff?"

"Only trainers would know that," Doug answered.

"Maybe he produces it in his cellar from a recipe in a book on black magic," I suggested.

"You'll never find out from Skip. He'll just turn on that pleasant who?-me? smile."

I thought that I had better take advantage of the beach-head that I had established with my own discomfort, so I explained to Jarrett directly, knowing that I was being over-heard by the others in the room, what I was there to do. Sensing that I had possibly made some gain and a little trust I nerved myself to go into the locker room where the men were dressing. Whenever a player emerged from the shower room I would follow him to his stall and introduce myself. Without exception I was received in a friendly way with what I believe was a minimum of reservation.

Several weeks later, when I flew to Chicago for a Sunday night game after I had been "bishopping" all day in Philadelphia I did not have time to exchange my clerical shirt and collar for mufti before arriving at the stadium.

This occasion not only surprised the unshockable reporters in the press box but illustrated to the team afterwards that I *was* a working bishop. Interestingly enough, my attire did not seem to be a barrier at all. They had become used to me regardless of what hat I happened to be wearing and nobody put on those special manners that are deferential to clergy.

On that first day of scrimmage when I stormed the dressing room, the ice was broken all around. It began to show upstairs at the lobby lunch where the reporters, the players, and I were congregating to be fed. The atmosphere was more relaxed. While I was quietly eating my lunch and not bothering anybody in particular, Lou Angotti sat down beside me.

"Is it true that you're a beepity-beep-beep priest?" he asked.

"Lou," I answered, seeing the players across the table about to go into convulsions, "it's even worse than that. I'm a bishop."

Without a pause he reached over and took the remains of a piece of watermelon and wore the rind as a headphone over his ears.

"Tell you what, Lou," I said laughing. "If you'll go to church with me, then I'll go out on the ice with you."

Angotti thought that over for a moment, then said, "What are you trying to do, get us both knocked off?"

While some of the men were in the "slumber room," or "recovery room," as I referred to it when we left the table this noon, I went back downstairs to the equipment room to resume getting acquainted. I watched the assistant trainer, Lou Vargas, sharpen a pair of skates for Nesterenko. I waited until Lou was finished before I introduced myself and went through my soft sell again. He listened attentively.

At length he asked me, "Will you do me a favor? For God's sake, spell my name right. It's *v-a-r-g-a-s,*" he spelled. "Everybody leaves off the *s,* and that isn't me."

I have seen many persons go through identity crises and I assured Lou that I didn't want to put him through one, so I would promise to get it right. "You think you have troubles, Lou? How would you like a name like Walter Tkaczuk of the New York Rangers and want people to get it right?"

"Yeah," said Lou, "and besides he wants it pronounced 'ka-chook,' like a Polish sneeze. Just the same, don't forget the *s*."

I asked Vargas if he minded if I snooped around the equipment room. "Go ahead," he said, "but don't lift anything."

"Not even a broken hockey stick?"

"For every one of those you carry out, that'll be ten bucks. The management has to stop somewhere on what can be taken out of here—and they made it 'nothing.'"

"What about the old ice skates?" I asked, thinking of the kids back home on Yardley Pond.

"Each guy buys his own, and they ride 'em right down to the rims and then give 'em to their kids or nephews and other relations. You'd be pretty far down the list."

Walking around the equipment room gave me the feeling that I was deep underground in a cave. It was complete with stalactites. Row after row of jerseys and long underwear were hanging from the ceiling. Along one wall were deep shelves holding pants, socks, garter belts (to hold their socks up after pulling them over the shin pads). There was a section filled with pads of all kinds, a bin full of pucks, shelves of tape, bandages, lotions—a combination drugstore and orthopedic appliance shop, including crutches.

There was a washer and dryer next to the machine shop where the repairs to skates and equipment were made. That place had everything except a place to sit down, so I went back up to the rink to see what was going on. As I came up the stairs from the hold, I heard the booming sounds of target practice that had already started.

The grind of training camp wore on. The day on which squad cuts would be made was getting closer. One could sense the mounting tension and each player's dread that he might be sent down. The main concern of the regulars was getting back into condition, or rather, getting back into shape. Keeping in condition means staying well, observing the rules of health, and seeing to it that the body receives proper exercise, nutrition, and rest. Getting in shape means sharpening one's reflexes and getting one's timing back after the summer period of disuse. Making the team didn't seem to be the primary problem of the veterans. The personal concern was whether or not one could recover last year's form, or even be better. Such nagging and doubting questions as, "Will I have a good year this year?" lay just below the surface of utterance. For example, Stan Mikita signed his contract late. A holdout since June, he missed only the first day of training camp. When he didn't appear Doug Mohns called him on the phone and asked him to come down and work out every day anyway, whether he had a contract or not. So Stan began working out with the squad. A systemic infection tagged him, and off he went to the hospital to find the source of the trouble. Would this mean a slow start for him this year? He wasn't the only one who was probably wondering about it. Would he equal last year's performance? Another unanswered question.

Pat Stapleton had crashed into the goalpost the previous February and had surgery which kept him out the rest of the season. Here it was September and he hadn't tried out his repair job. Would it hold? Would he be slowed down from last year? Another unanswerable.

Jim Pappin reported in at the stadium with a form of Bell's palsy, a painful condition which affects the eyesight and facial nerves on one side of the face. Even the breeze created by skating fast produced unimaginable pain. He tried wearing a thick pad of cotton to shield his cheek. This kind of condition had been known to linger with a person for weeks.

It's these things that try skaters' souls—and coaches' too. As if that were not bad enough, these men were all able and experienced veterans of ten years or more of the battle of hockey. They had many more miles on them than the twenty-year-old rookies. How much tread could be left? Endowed with abounding health and strength, men like Gordie

Howe have been able to play competitively in the League beyond their fortieth year, but there aren't many Gordie Howes. Eric Nesterenko and Doug Mohns at thirty-seven years showed signs of going on forever. But Bobby Hull calls himself the President and Founder of TANS. (There Ain't No Security). His fourteenth year in the League is coming up. How long can the strength and talent go before running out, or being hastened out by injury? These are the unknown variables of professional sports.

As I watched these men, veteran and rookie alike, skate around and around the rink getting in shape and sharpening their style and technique, I thought of the hours, days, and years of work that culminated in their grace and finesse. A little arithmetic reveals that by the time these men had become eighteen years old, they had spent over 10,000 hours on ice. How many miles would that total?

Dennis Hull recounted a scene from his boyhood at Pointe Anne, Quebec. "We lived in a town of about 300 people—a company town where everybody worked at the cement plant. There weren't enough boys of the same size and age to make up two teams, so a lot of times we'd all skate up the bay seven miles and get up a game with the Indian boys on the reservation. We'd play hockey all afternoon against them and then skate home for supper. I remember that it was only seven miles up there, but believe me, it was fifty miles back against a wind and the temperature around zero or below." You had to love hockey to do that.

I recalled during my days in Montana, when my work frequently took me across the border into the Canadian provinces of Alberta and Saskatchewan, that I would drive through those small prairie towns on bitterly cold, gray and windy days with blowing ground snow. Every hamlet had a place to ice skate. Often I would see two or three boys out on the ice banging a can around with a stick. Had I seen some of these men in their boyhood days on thses local ponds when the rest of the populace were at home sitting next to the fire? Even at night, driving through this winter wasteland, I invariably saw some boy out there in the frozen air, cutting wind and blowing snow, simply skating round and round in lazy circles. What makes a person do that? I have often wondered. I confessed this observation and meditation to some of the squad members. "Yes, I was probably one of them," they would reply with a smile and a faraway look in the eye of memory.

The coach's whistle signaled the end of the workout and scrimmage. Most of the skaters disappeared into the ice, back of the goal.

Five of them remained behind on the ice to do some private shooting practice. The workmen came down from the stands, where some of them had been "coaching," and began sawing and hammering the stands into opening-night condition. Other maintenance men resumed putting up the 6' by 3' panels of shatterproof glass above the board boundary of the rink. I took my handkerchief off of an exposed steel post having a sharp end that I had noticed at the beginning of scrimmage. Not wanting an impalement of any skater, especially where I was sitting, I took protective measures. There were a number of these steel supports against which the protective glass had not been placed, so I scrounged for rags to cover the ends for protection. I left my handkerchief on the post as evidence of my concern for the Black Hawks and ventured down on the ice, taking a station behind the goal and net. I crouched down so that I wouldn't be struck with a stray puck. Doug Mohns was practicing skating in on the goalie, Gerry Desjardins, at high speed for a one-on-one exercise. He accomplished this several times and I still couldn't figure out how he did it and how Gerry missed. I called Doug over to ask him if he and Gerry would do it in slow motion so that perhaps I could register what was happening.

In the meantime Pat Stapleton had returned to the ice after he had checked his last-season injury to his leg, and he was going around piling up miles. I was absorbed in watching the goal play and didn't see Pat coming at me from the left. He had been skating around unconcerned, pushing his hockey stick ahead of him sideways and piling up a ridge of shaved ice on it. As he came by, he lifted the stick and with a friendly smile dumped the ice on me.

"This is called 'deking' the opponent," called out Doug. He skated slowly from the point—the place where the blue line meets the board boundary of the rink. "Now watch as I skate in. I drop my shoulder and look like I'm going to drive a direct shot—Gerry moves out a little to cut down the angle —I fake the shot and after I go by him, tap it in with a back shot." And so he did.

"What if you hadn't gone out, Gerry?" I asked.

"Then he'd take the shot. It would be a much harder one and he'd have a good chance of making it. But in a game a defenseman is supposed to be coming in on the other side so Doug can't get off the backhand aftershot."

The praticing went on. I left them and went downstairs and watched Bobby Hull plane the edge of his hockey stick to his own specifications and liking. He would then put the stick under the hot-water faucet in the training room to soften it up for easy bending. The next step in the operation was to wedge the blade end in the cross supports of the training table and putting the right amount of stress on it to produce the desired curve. Bobby explained that only a half-inch curve is allowed now. He didn't seem too happy about it, and he told me why.

It came about in the 1961–62 season that Stan Mikita whacked at the puck in a workout and the stick broke verti-cally in the blade. He kept on using it because it was a practice session. He noticed the puck jumped a little when he took a shot, so that behaved like a pitcher's knuckle ball. "I was watching what was happening," Bobby said. "I tried a few shots and that puck really hopped. We decided to try to bend our own blades like you saw me do. For the next seven years Stan or me won the scoring championship. The NHL outlawed it, except for a half-inch curve."

He added that this "banana blade" had been reduced by

regulation to one-and-a-half inches in 1967, to one inch in 1968–69, and to a half-inch this year. The goaltenders complained loudly and long, saying that it was hard enough to stop the puck shot off a straight stick without adding curves and drops to its trajectory.

"I've been trying different sticks," said Hull, "but I haven't been able to adjust back to the straighter one. With the curved blade I could pull the puck in and then fling it. Now I have to stay with it longer and follow through, or I will slice the shot."

Stan Mikita also mumbles a lot about the restriction on the curve. "I've gotten so used to it that now with a straighter stick I'm having a hard time planing down the blade so that I can get the best lie on ice."

It was explained by Dennis Hull that even though it has cut down the scoring power of these two stars they are more of a threat than ever to the opposition. "This is because they roar down the ice and suddenly pass off to a teammate to take a shot while they go on down the ice for a rebound. Before the curve was reduced you knew that when these guys came down the ice and had a chance for a shot that they would take it and almost put a hole through the goalie or spin it around his neck. They're still deadly shooters, but most of the new men are pretty good at it, too, so now the defense has to set up for alternate defense. To the credit of both Stan and Bobby they pass oftener than they shoot, and we are still a high-scoring team."

After fifteen years in NHL competition they are wiser in their age. There's no waste motion. Now that Bobby and Stan look, fake, and pass, they form an offensive line. They hurt the enemy's play whether they shoot or not. And so go the observations and complaints of players who have to face these men.

The younger wing men are encouraged by Mikita. "Keep your stick on the ice and skate like hell. I'll get the puck to you," he counsels. And that's usually what happens.

The first exhibition game was an intrasquad affair

which included the Dallas farm team. This game really tightened up the rookies. It was their last chance. Only five of them would survive the exhibition schedule, and the final cut would be made at the season's opener against Oakland only two weeks away. An unnoticed and unfortunate accident occurred to one of the rookies who had come from Yugoslavia for a tryout. He skated accidentally into a flying puck whacked by Bill White, and his jaw was broken. After being wired together, he returned to his hotel room with his friends from overseas. These three young men could speak basic English, but being able to describe how food would have to be prepared for the unfortunate Anton was beyond anyone's capabilities.

Doug Mohns, the eighteen-year veteran with the Blackhawks, missed Anton and knowing that he had a broken jaw, searched him out and found him clinging to life by drinking milk shakes. Doug immediately took charge. Three days had gone by for Anton without anything else to eat and having no way of telling a waitress what his problem was—not knowing the American language—especially having to speak through a mouth that was wired shut. Mohns called up Pat and said that he was bringing Anton out to the apartment to be fed. Pat prepared a meal of steak, potatoes, vegetables, and everything—and ran it all through a blender. Anton was provided with an extra large straw for the happy occasion and dined immediately. These men fed him until his medical release was forthcoming, and his preparation for the return to his homeland had been completed—including a blender to take back with him.

Now that the season was at hand I was eager to follow the team on the long and difficult road that could lead to the great prize—the Stanley Cup and the world championship.

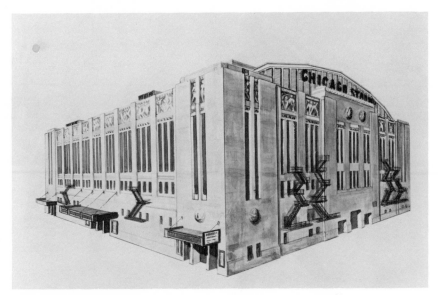

The fortress—Chicago
Stadium, home of the Black
Hawks, in a somewhat
idealized rendition.

General Manager Tommy Ivan
(*left*) and Coach Billy Reay.

What can
happen in
heavy traffic.
Bobby Hull
moves in on
goal amid
three defenders
(*this page,
above*); the
puck's gone,
but the goalie
is sliding into
the net (*this
page, below*)
and soon so
is Bobby
(*opposite
page*).

Hockey justice and injustice. Goalie Gerry Desjardins objects to a violation of territorial rights. Keith Magnuson (3) and Jerry Korab (22) skate in to set matters straight (*above*).

Magnuson and Korab lay down the law (*below*).

The issue becomes clouded as
the gloves go down. Magnuson
is ready for other comers
(*above*).

Now for the debate. Korab protests
innocence, but the stripe-shirted judge
(with armband) still renders his verdict.
As penalty times are assessed, Desjardins
observes with less emotion than the fans
(*below*). (*Chicago Tribune photos*)

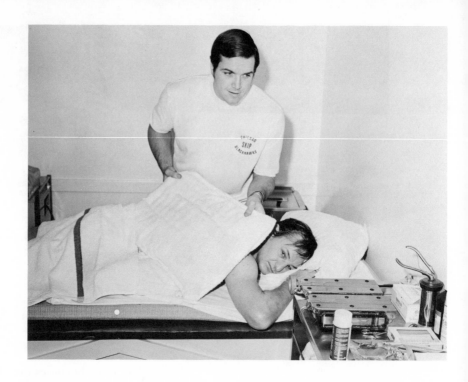

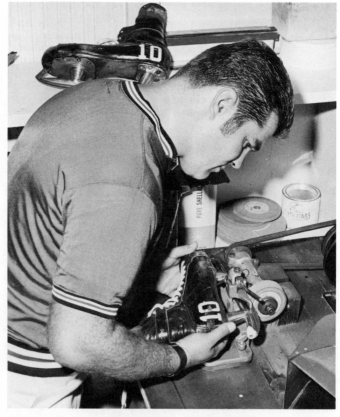

(*above*) Skip Thayer applying a heating pad to an aching Jim Pappin. (*Louis Okmun photo*)

(*opposite*) The sort of grind that can pay off. Lou Vargas hones a fine edge to Dennis Hull's skate.

An alliance worth keeping. Tony Esposito, with protective vest, and Bobby Hull, who makes goalies glad they have protective vests, in the days before the World Hockey Association. (*Louis Okmun photo*)

In a night's work. Pat Stapleton and "dueling scar."

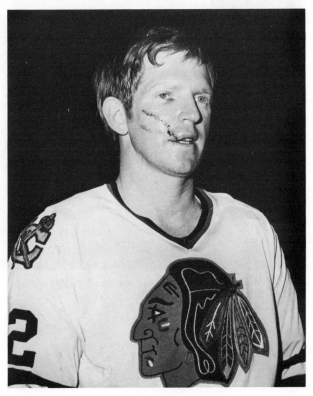

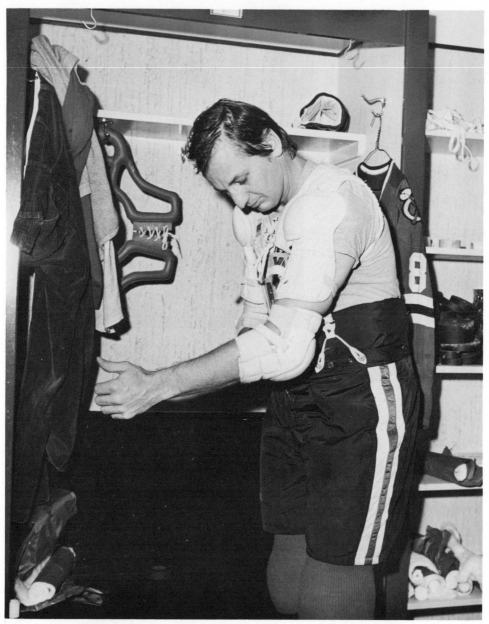

Why hockey players look bulky. Jim Pappin checks out his armor. (*Louis Okmun photo*)

Fame is nice, but . . . when
Stan Mikita skates in on goal,
special measures suddenly
seem necessary. In two
different games Stan was
hooked (*above*), and high
sticked (*below*), for being in—
for him—familiar territory.

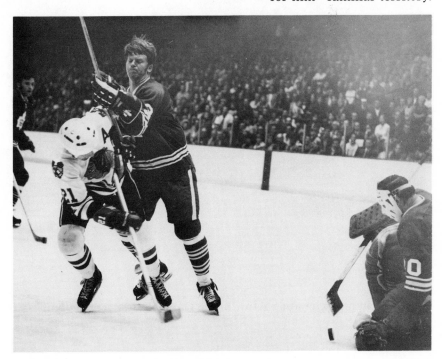

Stan Mikita and victim Bruce Gambel after a goal. 'Nuff said.

The value of a good forward
line. In a game against the
Canadiens, Dennis Hull (10),
Stapleton (12), and Koroll (20)
swarm the defense, with
Mikita about to swoop in for a
slap shot.

(*above*) The value of a good defense. Against the Canadiens again, Esposito handles both puck and an attacker while Magnuson (3), Campbell (14), and Nesterenko (15) cover the flanks.

(*opposite*) A moment to forget— if you can. Loose puck in front of the goal! Goalie Gary Smith watches anxiously as Cliff Koroll sees the threat and a Canadien sees an oppotunity.

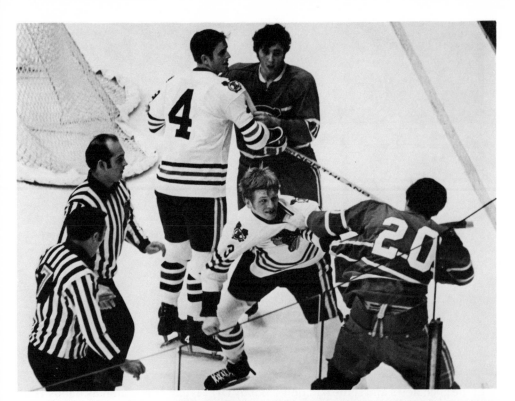

(*above*) A matter of judgment. Officials will sometimes let a fight go on if that will release explosive energy. Here Keith Magnuson (3) gets set to release.

(*opposite*) One way or another, it's going to hurt. Cliff Koroll is about to crash over a trip, and things are pretty grim higher up, too.

Some good news and some bad news. Bobby Orr (4) can only watch as Bobby Hull (*second from left*) sneaks the puck into the Bruin net. Keith Magnuson (3) gives the traditional salute. But in another game, Magnuson and Gerry Korab (22) have to bear watching the puck slip between Esposito's pads for an enemy score. (*Chicago Tribune photos*)

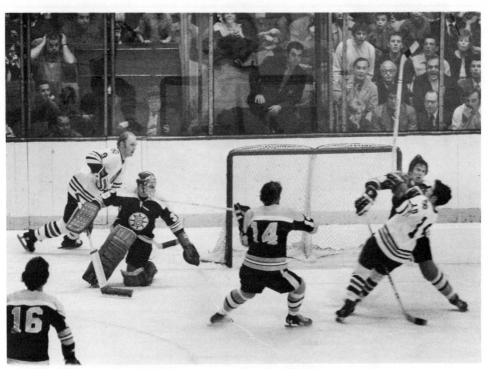

The crunch. Black Hawk Gerry Pinder is ganged by two Bruins deep in hostile country. (*Chicago Tribune photo*)

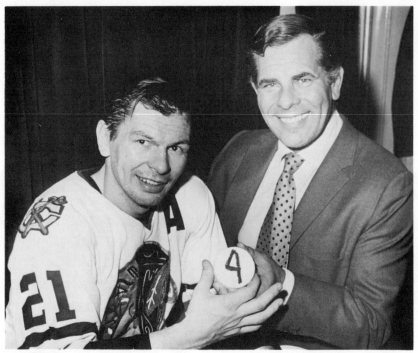

Hat Trick plus. Black Hawk
President Bill Wirtz
congratulates Stan Mikita for a
four-goal game.

While the fans headed for home, after
each victory, the press descended on the
Chicago locker room, and inevitably headed
for Bobby Hull.

7

We're All in This Together

●

In the early afternoon before the evening's scheduled game with Vancouver I walked into the training room on a matter of no more importance than hoping to find someone to talk to about hockey. There with one leg in the whirlpool bath stood a man whom I had not seen before. Skip Thayer introduced me to Art Skov, the referee assigned for the coming game. It was too early for the players to report in and dress for the game, but Art had shown up for a heat treatment on his leg. I began visiting with him.

Big-time sports officials had always been anonymous to

me, as I suppose they have been for others. Fans know certain ones by name, especially those who they remember as
having made decisions against the home team when they
were losing. As far as the fan is concerned the referees are
combusted on ice immediately before a game and dissolve
back into a limbo at the sound of the last whistle. During the
time that they are on ice they put up with crowd abuse. They
are loudly accused of incompetence, partiality, and blind-
ness. They are the targets of paper and plastic missiles and
vulgar suggestions recommending what ought to be done
with them and where they ought to go. It was in Chicago
Stadium that the organist, Al Melgard, was expressly forbidden to play "Three Blind Mice" on the pipe organ in agree-
ment with unhappy fans on an unpopular decision.

Art was not averse to talking about his job and way of
life. "Art," I asked, "I noticed that one of the three officials
wears a colored armband. Is that because he is the chief
referee for the game?"

"He is *the* referee," he explained. " The other two men
are linesmen. When you watch the game tonight you'll see
that each one is stationed at a blue line, mainly to watch for
offside—when a player skates across the line ahead of the
puck."

"The referee, I understand, is the one who decides on the
penalites, the offense, length of time, and so one. But the
linesmen are the ones who have to stop the fights. Sometimes they are in a big hurry to stop a fight and then at other
times they take their time. Why is that?"

"That's up to the linesmen and myself," Art said. "It's a
matter of using sanctified common sense. Sometimes it will
settle the teams down—take the pressure off so they can play
better hockey. It all depends. When we judge that a battle
has gone on long enough, one of us steps in between the men
and stops it." He smiled as he anticipated my next question.

"That's a pretty thankless part of the job," I observed,
dipping my hand in the whirlpool bath to see how hot the
water was. "You must be good fighters yourselves."

"We're all former hockey players, so we've had some experience," he explained, as he probably wondered just how dumb can the questions get.

"Where do hockey officials come from, other than having been former players?"

"They are scouted, as players are. They are developed slowly and most of us serve as trainee officials in a minor league. After some experience a man becomes eligible for spot assignments."

"I've watched officials work, and I've got to hand it to you. Every one of you are superb skaters. What I'm wondering about is, how long is an official's career? I would think that he runs out of gas before too many seasons."

"Oh," laughed Art "when your legs and reflexes slow down, then you've reached the end of the road. Most of us last into our early forties. Retirement has nothing to do with decline of competency, necessarily—just an inability to maintain the speed and pace of the game."

"And that's considerable," I said. "But getting back to a more cheerful aspect—how does one qualify as an official?"

"Well," he began, "you've gotta be in top physical condition and stay that way. You have to be a superior skater. Most officials learned early in their careers that they didn't quite have enough hockey talent for professional competition— maybe an inch short of what was necessary to hold their own against NHL standards. But they love the game, so they stay in it by turning to officiating. An official has to have basic good hockey sense and judgment. The referee sets the tempo and rhythm of a game pretty much by how much rough stuff he allows. He watches the face-offs to make sure that everyone is in his right place. He is also the final judge as to whether or not a goal has been scored."

"That's a big order," I commented. "How long are you going to keep your leg in the whirlpool?"

"It's long enough now. Any longer and I'd have a 'jelly-leg.' " He pulled it out and began drying off, preliminary to a massage. "I got caught against the boards the other night and have a mild charley horse." He walked over to the rubbing table and stretched out while waiting for Skip Thayer to complete the treatment.

As I watched Skip perform his healing arts, I thought to myself, "Art Skov is a happy-looking man. He's doing what he wants to do. He's got professional pride." I broke the silence, except for the low hum of Skip's vibrator that he was using on Art. "I understand the satisfaction of a job well done, but you fellows take a lot of heckling and shouting shrapnel from the fans. Take tonight, for instance. *Somebody* is bound to get angry. You're probably going to be accused of feeble-mindedness and partiality against the home team. How can you take it three and four nights a week?"

"It's part of the job, that's all," he smiled, along with unflappable Skip Thayer. "It's included in the price of the ticket—this right to give the officials the business."

I went upstairs, and as I did I walked past the closed door to the official's dressing room. A very official-looking sign announced: Officials Only. Admission by *anyone else absolutely forbidden.* "That's explicit enough," I reflected.

Don Murphy explained to me that a hockey referee makes more calls and decisions than a referee in any other sport except possibly baseball—if you include the balls and strikes. I learned that an official receives $17,000 for a seven-month season in which he travels over 75,000 miles a year and works in at least 70 games from coast to coast. Moreover, his assignments are made at least a month in advance, and no changes are ever made through pressure of management because of customer complaint. It takes a very real sense of vocation to stay on a job like that.

The spaces assigned for the Black Hawks business offices plainly were not planned. They happened. Out of the eight small rooms that made up the suite, there were only two that had any privacy where one could shut out the bustle and noise. The arrangement—if it could be called that—reminded me of old Victorian houses where one had to go through one or two rooms before arriving in the one you wanted. No matter where a staff member had a desk it was in a traffic pattern en route to another room. Murphy's office was directly off the elongated entry room which served as the reception space. The mailroom and statistician's office could be reached only by walking across Don's office. After sitting in Murphy's breezeway for a while, one got the idea that whatever was needed at any particular time by any of the staff could always be found in the mailroom—except the mail, of course, which was stacked on the long table in the entry.

The office of the Director of Public Relations was also the meeting place for everybody. First of all, it was the only room where one could sit down except at a desk. Appropriately there were eight chairs lined against the wall directly in the lane to the two rooms beyond the gathering place. On game nights the room was thronged with press representatives passing the time with each other while awaiting game time. Hats and coats were stacked in the next inner room where there was usually a photographer loading his camera and muttering to himself darkroom thoughts about clutter. When he made his break for freedom he was required to run the obstacle race over and around stretched-out legs of Don's relaxed press guests replaying last Sunday's game.

Murphy was an innkeeper, his office a way station between two points—the rink and the newspaper office. The place was never out of refreshments. When the chairs were filled the late arrivals perched on the massive table. The last man in sat on the Coke machine. Don presided over his court from his swivel chair and glass-topped desk expansively and with obvious pleasure. He was a gray-haired, jowled man whose body through natural aging in this mill was losing its battle against gravity; he also gave the appearance of having slept all night on the desktop, having loosened his tie and shoes. They were always loose but never off. Overall, he gave out the homey and disarrayed appearance of a bureau with the top drawer open. Before game time the

67

crowded room reminded me of a tree full of owls. To a new-comer and visitor they looked a bit predatory. One had to sit in the room with them for a while and soak up the sports world atmosphere before feeling at ease.

Without any signal that I could notice the caucus arose as one man at 7:20—fifteen minutes before game time—and filed out in approximate reverse order into the foyer en route to the press box. After making our way through the arriving fans up two flights of stairs, we were singly admitted to the "box" itself, a narrow lane about 50 feet long suspended from the balcony overhead and above the mezzanine seats. Beside the continuous "table" across the front which pro-vided work space, there were about 30 folding chairs. Cer-tain of these, by tradition and assignment, belonged to press veterans. The rest of the seats were catch-as-catch-can. At the far end of this suspension bridge was a table loaded down with food, presided over by a woman who prepared our plates according to our requests. Moreover you could make as many return trips throughout the evening as you wished. It was an excellent arrangement. It was also the busiest corner of the press box, the traffic pattern being as complex as Murphy's office.

Having loaded my plate and finding a seat that I trusted did not belong to a "regular," I sat enjoying the buffet and idly watching the crowd in the rapidly filling stadium. Sud-denly there was a roar exactly like that of the crowd in the *Ben-Hur* chariot-race scene. The Black Hawks were coming onto the ice. Al Melgard trumpeted their appearance on the organ as the skaters slowly circled the goal waiting for the Vancouver team to come on the ice. Vancouver arrived pres-ently and slight attention was paid to them. It is easy to see why visiting teams feel as though they don't have any friends. Later on in the game, when Vancouver scored, the 16,000 spectators remained silent. Tomorrow night at Olympia Stadium in Detroit I would find out, as a visitor, what it felt like for a crowd to make no comment when their team was scored against.

The Black Hawks scored eight times against Vancouver's two. The crowd and the team were ecstatic, but no one's joy was matched by Dan Maloney's delight. The rookie who came up from the London, Ontario, Knights, and survivor of training camp scored two goals. The first goal of his NHL career was also the first one in this game. I didn't have an opportunity immediately after the game to congratulate him because of the crowd of reporters surrounding him in the dressing room. Besides, I was busy earning my way to Detroit.

Having inquired previously of Don Murphy what the number of the flight to Detroit was—and the airline—I had made my reservation so that I could accompany the team. My immediate problem was getting to the airport. The flight was scheduled to leave at 11:15 P.M., only an hour and a half after the game with Vancouver was over. The team members drove their own cars to the airport, some of them in previously arranged car pools, while the others were taken out by their wives. I was too new at this to intrude upon what might be routine arrangements. I mentioned my problem to Skip Thayer. He invited me to ride out on the stadium service car with him and Lou Vargas, and all the equipment. So, after the game I went immediately to the equipment room and began loading the gear in the truck with them.

The system was impressive. When the team returned to the dressing room after the game there was a 5'-long zipper bag in front of each cubicle. The numbers on the bags coincided with the cubicle number as well as the number on each piece of equipment and uniform of every player. As the men undressed for showers, each piece was dropped into their numbered gear bag except for their jerseys. The red ones that they wore for home games were replaced by the white jerseys for the road. As soon as a bag was zipped shut, Lou would carry it to a dolly and stack it there. A full load was then transferred to the truck. Within ten minutes from the end of the game all the gear was on the truck, ready to be taken to the airport. The players weren't even out of the showers yet. Skip and Lou took their seats alongside the driver and I climbed in amid the gear.

The underground passageways of the stadium weren't designed for panel trucks. Slowly the driver made his way around the workmen who were already taking the sections of the basketball court to assemble for the next day's basketball game. The truck crawled up the steep ramp and through the crowd of young fans waiting in the parking lot for autographs from the night's heroes who had not as yet appeared for their hurried ride to the airport.

"What are you going to do with the gear when you get to Detroit?" I asked as we rumbled along the expressway. "Will there be a panel truck waiting?"

"Yeah," said Lou. "We go from the airport to the stadium and hang up the equipment before we go to the hotel."

"Then you fellows won't get to bed until about four A.M.," I guessed.

"Right. No sleep on the road in this business."

"What time do you go back to the stadium tomorrow?" I asked, trying to figure ahead of time how I would get out there from the hotel. I had already decided to go directly to the hotel with the team, if I could get on their bus.

"We're going out about three in the afternoon and set up," said Skip. "We'll take a cab out, if it's a ride you're thinking about."

"I'll see what's going on tomorrow afternoon. If I see you around I may go along."

Arriving at the airport we drove directly to the ramp where the plane was being loaded, put all the gear aboard, walked around to the passengers' entrance and made our way to the proper gate. The team was gathering there, each man having his own small overnight case. Some of them looked up in surprise when they saw me with Skip and Lou. Seeing Dan Maloney standing there, I went up to him and praised him for his first two goals in NHL competition. He looked as happy as a young boy with a new red bicycle.

The flight was called and the team queued up and went

aboard. At this time of seating I had no way of knowing what the seating customs and habits of the team were, so I came aboard last. Well, almost last. Bobby Hull had a reputation to uphold, and that was to step aboard the plane as the door closed. So I was next to last. Never in his career with the Black Hawks has he ever been known to brush off an autograph seeker. He always has time for anyone, even though the team may be yelling at him from inside a bus to get moving. Doug Jarrett suggested that they ought to have a theme song for departures called "Waiting for Bobby."

Those who played cards sat three abreast, prearranged I'm sure, so they could pick up from where they left off on the last trip. Some others, as soon as they were belted in, immediately started napping. Gerry Desjardins was sitting alone at the window, so I moved in with him and took the vacant aisle seat with his nodding consent, leaving the seat between us unoccupied. I noted that Tony Esposito, who had goaltended the night's game was already stretched out with eyes closed and enjoying some peace without any pucks flying at him. He was also sitting alone. I wondered if all goalies everywhere sat alone and lived apart from their teammates.

I had read somewhere that a goalie in hockey may be compared to a catcher in baseball, mainly, I suppose, because he has his glove on the elusive and sought-after object oftener than anyone else. But there seems to me to be more of a similarity between a goalie and a baseball pitcher, certainly as far as his attitudes and psychological conditioning are concerned.

Both baseball and hockey are contrived to make life miserable for either pitcher or goalie. To a degree, a quarterback in football is vulnerable to the same reactions, but he gets to sit down once in a while when his team is on defense. The goalie isn't part of a platoon system. His world is always in an imminent state of collapse. In football the quarterback's desire is to throw the ball to a receiver. He objects strenuously to anyone who has the bad manners to break up

71

a play. The pitcher in baseball tries to get the ball into the catcher's mitt. But a succession of men stand between the pitcher and the catcher, each batter in turn trying to break up the game of catch. This requires a pitcher to be crafty and sly. Naturally he is upset when a batter slams what he considers an excellent pitch out of the park. There are times in the life of a pitcher when opposing batters are obviously ganging up on him. The catcher pleads for him to put the ball in the mitt. A pitcher is a strange cat. His talent and profession have made him into a person different from other men.

In hockey the goalie suffers parallel misfortunes and rejections. He knows that the enemy is interested only in filling *his* net with pucks. They are out to shoot him down. Although the goalie has five teammates on the ice to help him get the puck away from the opposition, still what will they do with the puck when they gain control? They'll reverse the field and skate off to plague the other goaltender. The goalie is a brother member of the fraternity of security guards. What can other players really know about suffering? He can too easily deduce that all hockey players who are not goalies exist simply to plague goalies. It can make one paranoid.

To some readers all this may seem overdrawn, but one must remember that there is a surprisingly large number of persons in this world who have a very active fantasy life. Goaltenders are of this remarkable subspecies, even as are pitchers and quarterbacks. It is an occupational risk of these highly exacting professions. It may be part of what makes them great and enables them to withstand the buffets of their lives. Call it rationalizing. Call it what you will, it remains a strong contributing factor to their proficiency in their vocations.

Goalies have more occupational risks than other players. They suffer variously from indigestion, colitis, insomnia, and high blood pressure. These are but a few of the disorders that have psychosomatic overtones which afflict them. "Puck shock" can trigger off alarming symptoms. An example is the goalie who was being driven home after the game by his wife. Six goals had been scored against him that night. He slumped in the front seat in a state of exhaustion, a beaten man. His wife came to a sudden stop at a red blinker light. He looked up out of his syncope and saw the red light blinking at him like the one in the arena had done six times that night. His reflex told him that he had been scored on again. With a strangled yell he leaped over into the back seat of the car, "Keep that puck out of here!"

His wife reported that after the first attempt she didn't try to get him to climb back in the front seat but let him lie there in prenatal position all the way home. He had about as much poise as a treed cat.

I asked a goalie if he could be trusted to drive a car during a stressful season. There was an admission that a flasher light on a patrol car could sometime trigger off a defensive reflex action. Oncoming fire trucks were the real test of courage. If they were noisy enough the goalie could reflex out in front of it to frustrate the attack.

May the Great Goalkeeper in the skies preserve the cop who tries to make a goalie pull over to the side if the athlete is driving home after just giving up six goals. He just might go after the fuzz just as he repulses the left wing. Even the red light on the oven at home has been known to produce a reflex action. Prizefighters have been known to become punch-drunk from their trade. Stories are told about the old days, when street cars were in bloom, about the boxer who came up swinging every time he heard the bell clang on the tram. Goalies go into puck shock. It is the great danger in their occupation. It feeds paranoia. Being a goalie he already has more than enough of that than his family can tolerate.

There is a degree of tension in goalkeeping that exceeds even that of a pitcher or quarterback. All three of these men have heavy responsibilities. But the pitcher gets a rest every three outs and the quarterback has time off to recover when the defensive unit is on the field. Moreover, the pitcher seldom works more than every fourth or fifth day, and the quarterback once a week. The goalie will average four games a week without any let-up during the entire game. If you played goalie that often, your fantasy-life would be considerably enriched, too—in a nightmarish sort of way.

Then there is the fear factor in goaltending that has become common in the modern speed-up game. Several times during a game five opponents come charging down the ice, eyes glistening, and shouting threats. They try to establish a state of chaos in front of the net. The aim of this confusion is to dogpile the goalie and sneak the puck into the net. His own teammates ride over the hill to the rescue to clear the ice of these invading Huns. The milling about of the enemy plus the dispersal tactics of his teammates produce a situation in which a shot may be made at the goal which the goalie can't see. This is politely and reverently known as a screen shot. Often the first inkling that the goalie has where the puck is he gets by the flashing red light. The screen shot is just plain dangerous. The goalie lives with the ever-present possibility of stopping a shot with his face, a shot that he never saw coming.

A third contributing factor to a goalie's susceptibility to psychic trauma is the 30-plus pounds of armor that he has strapped on him. He lumbers about the entrance to his cave, his mobility encumbered. He hides apprehensively inside the carapace. He lurks inside his vestments waiting for the day of wrath. The anxiety of the situation would make a brass ape shiver. Tony Esposito testifies that the supreme frustration for him is his inability to take off after a marauding opponent, chase him down the ice, and high-stick him through the ice down to the freezing coils. But he has to stay behind and watch the store. His sole relief comes from watching the enemy get his comeuppance from one of the defensemen.

Now in case you think that all this is overdrawn, let me cite the well-known reaction of Jacques Plante, one of the all-time goalie greats. He always came down with a severe attack of asthma whenever he played in Toronto, but never anywhere else. He tried to ease the problem and the symptoms by staying in a motel outside the city and arriving at the Maple Leaf Gardens just in time for the game. He also noted that when he played against Toronto on his home ice that he didn't have any symptoms. Behold, it is all a great mystery which is beyond the understanding of anyone but a goalie.

Goaltending is a lonely business. Watch him when the play is elsewhere. He knows that the wandering horde will return. After the melee his team goes roaring down the ice abandoning him to his solitude and meditations and apprehensions. Even when the mob is clamoring at the gates he is the lonely man in the crowd. He doesn't do things the other players do.

It is no wonder that goalies are isolates and have a reputation for being difficult to talk to and almost impossible to live with. There is a hermit and ascetic quality to their lives. In front of their netted caves, transformed by their carapaces, they become holy lobsters of the desert ice—a mixed metaphor indeed. But so is the goalie.

The gentle bump of the landing brought everyone back into this present world, including the two slumbering goalies. Slowly, and still in a drowse, we completed the long walk to the waiting bus. I rode with the team downtown to the hotel. Finding myself seated again alongside Gerry Desjardins I decided to engage him in conversation, but thought better of it at the time. I took a paperback out of my pocket and started to read. Gerry, casting a sidelong glance, possibly curious about my reading tastes and preferences, asked me what I was reading.

"*Stalking the Wild Asparagus.* It's about the preparation and cooking of wild food that sometimes grows in vacant lots and can be found anywhere in the woods or on the prairies." I explained a little about how acorn flour is made, how to cook burdock and make dandelion coffee.

"Did you ever try any of that stuff?" he asked, becoming curious and probably beginning to suspect that I might be a food faddist.

"This is the first that I have ever read about such things. I find it interesting, that's all," I said.

"Thinking even about acorns makes me hungry," Gerry commented.

"Me too. Do you happen to know if there's any place open at the hotel at this time of night?"

"There's a place about a block away. Some of the guys will probably go over for a snack, but not me, much as I'd like to."

"You seem to me to be one of those fellows who gain and lose weight easily," I ventured.

"Mostly *gain*. I can put on 5 pounds almost overnight, so I have to watch my weight. If I go above 185 pounds my game falls off. The only time that I can really eat safely is right after I've tended goal for a game. That takes off about 5, so then I have some leeway. But I watch it."

I thought it best to get off the subject of food with this man who had a daily battle limiting his intake. Directly behind us was sitting Cliff Koroll, who had become interested when he overheard our conversation. "Do you have any more books in your briefcase?" he asked.

"Oh yes," I answered. "An alcoholic likes to be near his next drink when he needs it—or thinks he does. I'm that way about reading."

We were about to get into a conversation that I anticipated would lead us far afield when I noticed that the bus driver had begun circling around downtown one-way streets and spiraling in on the hotel. This could be called "unfinished business" which I might be able to pick up with him at a later date, so we left it there.

We filed out of the bus and into the hotel lobby. As each person came to the desk the keys to the assigned rooms were given out. Within three minutes everybody had disappeared but me. I had no reservation and had to trust to luck. The desk clerk assumed that I was not with the team but had simply followed them into the lobby. He looked me over as though I might have a suitcase full of narcotics. By now it was nearly two o'clock in the morning and I didn't care particularly what he suspected as long as I could have a room. By the time that I had registered and had been escorted to the elevator I met some of the team members coming out of the one that I was waiting for. So that settled the question for me about going out to grab a bite. I was so tired anyway that I didn't even try to resist my poor timing and misfortune at having missed the excursion for a snack. It was the sack for me.

8

Roadwork

●

Morning arrived mercifully late in Detroit. I came into the lobby about ten o'clock to seek out the coffee shop. Having missed last night's snack I was over-ready for breakfast. Escorted to a small table by the hostess-cashier, I was seated next to a dignified lady whose interesting features revealed the combination of age, wisdom, and intelligence. However, she was no more gaunt nor eroded than our shared waitress who looked enough like her to be her sister. Being more interested in coffee and breakfast, in that order, at the time, I did not meditate on the principles of affinities or correspondences. But by the time that I had finished my breakfast I was involved in both subjects, to the amusement and curiosity of the Black Hawks who were seated within watching and listening distance.

While I was drinking my morning first-cup and waiting for the eggs and bacon, my neighbor spoke up. "Are you by any chance here for the bridge tournament?" she asked.

"Why, no, I'm not," I answered. "I didn't know that there was one here today."

"There isn't," she explained. "It's over at Cobo Hall, and this hotel being nearby and traveling men home for the weekend, I supposed that the hotel was filled with people who were going to play in the tournament. There are over 400 people signed up—that's 100 tables," she added.

"I suppose that they come from around the state," I ventured.

"Farther than that," she informed me. "They come from Indiana, Ohio, and Ontario, Canada, as well. I'm from Ashtabula."

"Tell me," I urged in curiosity, "did you come with a 'team' or a couple or four of you or however it is?"

"I came alone. My late husband and I started coming to these tournaments five years ago. I have kept on with it because I find it stimulating and enjoyable. It gives me something to do."

"God love ya," said the waitress who was serving us both during this conversation. "I'm a two-time widow myself. And I find waiting on tables is stimulating and enjoyable, too. I don't have to do this, because I'm keeping a home for my 89-year-old stepfather, and it gets me out with people."

"*Eighty-nine* years old!" exclaimed the bridge lady. "And he doesn't need you at home all the time to take care of him?"

"Heavens, no, honey. He does the shopping and goes to see his friends every day. It was only last year they wouldn't renew his driver's license."

"I think that's wonderful!" the bridge lady answered.

"That's the way my husband lived—and he passed away last year at the age of 83. He always said that when you sit around the house in old age, you get to be a bed case and hang around forever. Everett saw to it that would never happen, and he had me jumping all the time and I'm twenty years younger than he was."

I felt jerked in my seat as though we had turned a sharp corner. The waitress, motioning with her eyes and head, asked, "Who do you think those nice-looking young men are here in the dining room?"

The bridge lady scanned the immediate horizon. I watched the faces of the Black Hawks, who by now were in this as deep as I was—innocent bystanders. "Say, they are fine-looking boys," she observed. "Don't tell me they're here for the bridge tournament."

"They're the Chicago Black Hawk hockey team. They stayed here last night and they're playing the Red Wings tonight at the stadium," the waitress explained.

"That can't be the same place as Cobo Hall, can it?" she asked worriedly, as if she was picturing a combination of bouts.

"God love ya, honey, the Olympia Stadium is clear across town. I take the bus by there on my way to work." The waitress broke off the conversation to serve "those nice-looking young men."

The bridge lady finished shuffling her toast and dealing out assorted pills for herself. The table conversation ended with the bowing out of the waitress, so I assumed that she had already begun to think about the mental rat-mazes of bridge and the bringing of order out of chaos at the card table. She too, as are hockey players, was devoted to order— each of their version. She left a tip, picked up her check, bade me good-by with an invitation to visit the tournament and happily went forth to trump.

The nearest table of Black Hawks gazed and grinned at me. I shook my head in mock confusion, picked up my cup and saucer, and joined them. "God love ya, honey, but you were sure patient with those old girls," laughed Doug Jarrett. "C'mon, sit in," he added as room was made for me by "those nice-looking young men" who were hopefully here for the bridge tournament.

Besides Dennis Hull and Keith Magnuson at the table, the fourth at "breakfast bridge" was Cliff Koroll with whom a conversation had started on the bus last night. He was now in his second, or sophomore, year with the Hawks. He had been a teammate and fellow All-American in collegiate hockey at the University of Denver with Keith Magnuson, who also roomed together at home and on the road. Dennis Hull roomed on the road with Doug, the court jester for the day. Keith is the "club policeman" who steps into every fight when he's on the ice just to "help out." ("I help persuade the League bullies to leave my friends alone, especially those who aren't so handy with their dukes.")

Dennis is expected to exceed his brother because he's five years younger. His style of play is so different from Bobby's that the unperceptive fan not only expects the wrong things from Dennis but is always reminding him of it. Yet, he is one of the fastest skaters in the League and anybody's equal on ice. He doesn't bask in Bobby's light and has yet to score a hat trick in big-league competition. (He told me on another occasion later that he was beginning to think that he would end his career some day being the only 500-goal scorer in League history who didn't do a hat trick.) Time after time Dennis scores two goals in a game—and a lot of assists. The team knows his value, and Dennis loves the game.

"Who was that lady I seen you with?" Doug quipped.

"That was no lady. She was a bridge player," I said. "You know full well that she was," I added accusingly.

Cliff had another matter on his mind. "What kind of a book are you doing about us?" he asked directly. Suspecting that he had in mind a possible "exposé" book, I answered him forthrightly. Somewhere along the line, things were getting turned around. I was the one being interviewed. But

I suppose that this kind of book was certainly suspect as far as the team was concerned.

"You've done a lot of reading, haven't you?" observed Keith. I admitted it, recalling last night.

"How do you know what to read?" pressed Koroll. "I like to read, too, but I've almost giving up finding anything. I can't get interested in the junk on the newsstands or in drugstores."

"The best places to get books are the big-time bookstores or the book department of the downtown stores. They have almost anything you could ask for."

"Yeah, but what do I ask for?" pursued Cliff.

"You are a university graduate, aren't you?" I teased.

"So what?" cut in Magnuson. "My college work was in physical education and business administration. Cliff and I have college educations but we don't know much. Sort of specialists, I guess."

"I'm the one that's dumb around here," confessed Dennis. "High school was 'it' for me. And even then I had hockey on my mind all the time."

"It isn't a question of being bright or dumb," I explained. "It's a matter of being informed and knowledgeable on things you might become interested in. A college education doesn't provide that for anyone."

"I think we all want to know, but I for one don't know how to go about it," Cliff concluded.

"Would you like to have me make out a list of books that you might find interesting?" I asked. "I'll have to make a guess as to what your tastes and interests are."

"You can leave out the sex books," Cliff said. "You practically get hit over the head with them every time you pass a newsstand."

"Yeah, read one and you've read 'em all," added Dennis.

"That'll be good," agreed Doug. "When you're on the road you sure get sick of watching television in your room or going downstairs and being a lobby lizard."

I promised them a reading list as soon as I returned

home and applied myself thoughtfully to the subject. What *does* one suggest to a professional hockey player for reading material? I decided on the "shot-gun method," that is, to cover as wide a range as possible because oftentimes a push-off from the dock of curiosity is all that's needed to start casting for the fish of knowledge and understanding.

Since breakfast was over, and after frequent glances at our twice-widowed waitress who was becoming a little impatient with our dallying into the lunch hour, we gathered up our individual checks and headed toward the cashier's desk. Awaiting our turns I said, "I'm going over to the big downtown department store in about an hour. If anybody wants to go along I'll be your guide and conductor through the book jungle."

"We'll meet you in the lobby, O.K.?"

"Around one."

Having nothing whatever to do except await the convenience of whoever planned to make the excursion to the bookstore with me, I took a chair in the lobby to indulge in people-watching. When one sits in a lobby for a few minutes the tempo and rhythm of lobby life emerges, and one begins after a while to notice things that are overlooked or ignored by the casual stroller.

Over there sits the husband waiting for his wife to join him in walking over to the bridge tournament. He looks like a bridge player. Wrong again. Two men come in off the street and join him. They leave in haste together.

That attractive young woman sitting over there is looking at her watch every thirty seconds. Is her husband going to be lectured for tardiness when he arrives? Or does her looking at every new face reveal her apprehension that she may recognize someone, or worse yet, that *she* may be recognized at noon in a downtown hotel lobby? A first lover, perhaps? It is all a great mystery.

A platoon of puck-chasers files through the revolving door. I wonder idly if a goalie would like that kind of entrance to his goal. Beginning to understand the meaning of foyer fatigue, I stand up for a stretch.

Here come Skip Thayer the trainer, and Lou Vargas, his "Watson." We stand there and visit. I learn that Thayer received his Bachelor of Science degree from the University of Maine, worked for his Master's at the University of Indiana, and did two years of college teaching before joining the Black Hawks.

"How did you ever line up with a job like this?" I asked him.

"The usual series of coincidences, I guess," Skip answered. I heard that the job was vacant, so I applied for it, not really expecting anything to come of it. I figured that the list of applicants would be long."

"I have already noticed that you seem to like the job," I noted. "For myself, I sometimes think that I'm a frustrated college professor. I would like teaching on the college level."

"I'm a frustrated athlete," he answered. "All desire and no talent. I find professional sports the biggest challenge and risk that a man in my business can take."

"You know that I've been hanging around your one-room hospital, or intensive-care ward," I said, "but I'm just beginning to find out what a trainer does. I've seen the first aid to injured and the ministry to sore muscles, but what else is involved?"

"Well, a large part of the job is the tending to the needs of twenty or so athletes who are seldom without physical problems of some degree seven days a week. It means being on hand at all times," he explained. "Then I supervise rehabilitation under the M.D.'s direction if the injury has been serious enough to take him out of action. When a doctor says a player is ready for exercise, then I take over and run things."

"You could use a pilot's license," I commented, "what with all those therapeutic devices available—diathermy, ultrasonic whirlpool, and that fiery stuff labeled 'Atomic Balm.' I'm going to have to watch and see how you smear

that on the victim-patient without going up in flames yourself."

Skip just smiled. Then I asked him how and when he
and Lou went out to Olympia Stadium to get ready for the
night's game.

"We go out by cab, the two of us. If you want to ride
along, meet us here in the lobby about three o'clock."

I still had time to conduct the bookstore tour. My tour-
ists had arrived and were standing across the lobby waiting,
so I said that I'd meet the trainers at three o'clock on this
spot. Then we took off on the field trip. About an hour and
a half later we returned supplied with readable paperbacks
on a variety of subjects.

We arrived at the stadium early enough for me to pick
up my press pass for the evening without any confusion. To
my surprise the visiting team's dressing room was easy to
find here. Usually they are hidden away in the dungeon area
as in the Colosseum of ancient Rome, so faithfully copied by
the architect who designed the Chicago Stadium.

I tried the door and found it unlocked, which surprised
me. But then, it was only about 3:30 in the afternoon and the
building had a tomblike quiet to it. I went in and found Skip
and Lou "setting the table." That is, they were laying out
strips of plastic containing air bubbles. I was patiently told
that these were used to wrap around the top of the ankles
where the shoelaces were tied. There was adhesive tape
strung like streamers from the table. There was a large box
of chewing gum—enough to accommodate a teen-ager for a
week. The uniforms, pads, and other equipment that the
skaters wore were suspended from hangers in front of each
cubicle. Vargas was standing the hockey sticks in a row
along the wall near the door. Each stick had the player's suit
number on it—three of them for each man, and each one
tailor-made and previously worked on by the user to suit his
own preferences.

Sidestepping Lou, who was coming past with a huge
armload of towels, I sat down in Bobby Hull's cubicle. Noth-

ing much happened to me. I felt no surge of talent or strength. Lou barged by and gathered an armload of hockey sticks to take out to the bench at the start of the game for possible and necessary replacements. Lou said that three or four sticks are broken during a game, not over opponent's heads but because of hard shots or in "digging" the puck out of corners and off the boards. A stadium attendant brought in a large urn filled with a thirst-quenching drink. Lou transferred some of it into a couple of half-gallon plastic bottles and screwed on caps fitted with long tubes like soda straws, also to be taken to the players' bench.

I mention this because I have heard a spectator ask his neighbor what the goalie skated over to the bench to get a drink of—as though he suspected that it might be liquid pep pills. I asked Skip about drug use in hockey. In his quiet way Skip answered that these fellows don't use any of the "bennies" or "greenies." They're high enough when they get out there, I gathered. Cliff, among others, believes that drugs actually throw off timing and coordination and that body-produced adrenalin does the job of stimulating better. I also asked the trainer why they didn't keep a small oxygen tank and mask at rink-side. It was explained that the offensive line is replaced at regular intervals just short of making such "stuff" necessary. And that was that.

All this may be difficult for the jaded American sports fan to believe. He hears and reads constantly about drug use in American sports and accepts it as part of that way of life. One must bear in mind that all but a meager handful of hockey players are Canadians and did not grow up and develop as athletes with American sports values. They are aliens to America in this sense, and although the national cultures are quite similar, still the Canadian athlete is distinctly different from his American brother. Canadian athletes haven't adopted these practices, mainly for reasons stated above as well as their further shrewd observation that athletes who do use stimulant drugs simply don't last as long in competition.

Even hockey injuries are different from those in other sports. The hockey player has muscle bruises and charley-horse problems. Knee injuries occur usually as a result of collisions with the iron goalpost. Not wearing cleats on skates means that the foot, not being anchored, places little stress on the knee joint. Having stitches taken is a way of life with hockey men. Upon my first acquaintance with the sport I expected to see heads and faces that were hen-tracked with suture marks. But the scars of battle don't show—except for an occasional displaced nose that has been broken and moved about the face during a career. It usually ends up with a permanent swelling across the bridge. Several men, I note, have permanent bruise marks, or "smile-scars," on the neck or biceps as a result of having been chopped down sometime in their career. Pulled shoulder muscles resulting from being roughed up along the boards while digging for the puck are a common injury.

Concussions and skull fractures happen occasionally but not as frequently as one might think. It is a saying that all a guy needs is either one of the two injury experiences and he sees the true light and adopts the helmet. If this is any index of the frequency of serious head injuries, then it is surprising that there are so few in view of the total amount of ice time of all hockey players. The rate is very low. The wearing of face masks by goalies became almost a necessity for survival with the development of the screen shot where the goalie can't see what's happening to the puck and often doesn't find out until he feels the bullet impact on his mask.

I was learning much today. The players began to show up, so I removed myself from the dressing room because I did not know the ground rules concerning the presence of an outsider. I presumed that like everybody else, hockey players also have individual scruples, superstitions, and hang-ups about their work and the circumstances under which they prefer to do their job.

Going out into the maze of halls and runways of this vast

cave, I watched the concession employees setting up their stands, warming up the hot dogs and making the coffee as they prepared for the thundering herd of fans who would begin arriving soon.

The officers of the law were amassed in a double row in the main lobby, peeling off to their assignments upon the lieutenant's order. A tier of ushers made their way to their appointed aeries. On my way to the pressroom for my pre-game snack I stopped to observe a hawker prepare his felt-covered board with pennants, miniature hockey sticks, and plastic buttons with all kinds of "messages" on them. He was fishing his wares out of a small closet underneath the stands. A huge supply of the official hockey magazine was already stacked on his small table.

"Getting all set to go to work?" I asked when it was perfectly obvious to both of us that that's what he was doing.

"Yup," he answered, "but I'm not open for business yet."

"I'm not ready to buy yet, anyway," I answered defensively. "How do I get to the pressroom from here?"

"See this here ramp?" he instructed. "Don't go up it. Just look out from there to the far end. Then look up to the mezzanine. You'll find it up there somewhere, but you go around to the other end before climbing."

"Thank you," I said. I continued to stand around, but out of his way. "Is this your spot right here?"

"Yup. Had it for eleven years now. I work every night that something's going on here."

"This isn't your only job, is it?" I asked.

"Hell, no, it ain't. I got a gas-station job daytimes, but with a wife and four kids and Ma, I got to scramble all the time. I got a good deal here. On at six-thirty, off at ten after checking in. Don't lose no sleep and don't have to run my ass off filling tanks and besides I get outa the nuthouse at night." He didn't even look up from his work as he explained his way of life so lucidly. Here's a man, I thought, who is the realist, and knows exactly what he's doing—and a man of few illusions.

The game against the Red Wings was a seesaw affair with a short board and more "saw" than "see." A 2–1 decision for the Black Hawks was not as decisive as desired, from their point of view. Bobby Hull slammed in a slap shot. Pit Martin stole the puck and raced down the ice, scoring in a one-on-one situation between himself and the goalie—and that was it. The passing of the puck was off, the pass seeming always just out of reach. The skaters were either too far ahead of it and were called for offside, or too far behind it and then the puck was intercepted. Art Skov, the referee, had explained to me that they can tell how good a team is by how accurately they pull up to the blue line without crossing it. The Black Hawks weren't "on" with their timing yet, but this was only the third game of the season. To the player the answer always is "more ice time."

After the game I made my way through the crowd gathering at the dressing room door for autographs and was allowed in by the guard. There was more relief than elation at having won. Everybody understood that more work was necessary. "It's going to be a tough year," said Bobby Hull who had been double-teamed much of the time. "Everybody'll be up against us because of last year." It looked like he was right.

I walked to the entrance off the street to see what the chances were of getting a ride back to the hotel. Several of the players had friends and acquaintances waiting for them at the curb to take them to a postgame party. I came upon Larry Romanchyk, a twenty-one-year-old tryout rookie for center, standing there alone.

"Going back to the hotel?" I asked. "Or are you waiting to be picked up by friends?"

"To the hotel," Larry answered. "I don't know anybody here to party with."

"Me too. Mind if I share a cab, that is, if we can get one?"

After we managed to hail a taxi and settled in for the ride downtown, I asked Larry how everything was going.

"I think I'm being sent down," he confessed. "It's a kind

of relief, in a way. I've been running scared all through training season wondering when they were going to get to me. It's down to Dan Maloney, Ray McKay, and me, now. It doesn't look good."

"You're only twenty-one aren't you?"

"Yes. As I say, I don't mind it too much because I know that I need the experience. This has been a rough time, you know, playing with fellows like the Hulls, Mikita, and the other regulars. They're all nice and helpful and all that, but what it does is make me anxious about whether I'm playing right or not. The worst of all is knowing that you're being watched and never knowing whether you're getting a good mark or a bad one. The hard part about it is that I have a wife and our baby daughter in Flin Flon waiting to hear from me, and I haven't anything to tell her—yet."

This is what happens to the young men attempting to make it in big time. The waiting around for weeks, sometimes, and working your heart out and wondering what they are going to do with you—and when.

9

Is This Seat Taken?

●

I planned to meet the team in December when they took their next road trip east. They would play against the Rangers in Madison Square Garden and the next night in the Spectrum in Philadelphia, making it four games in six nights. Now that the season was in full swing and the team averaging three games a week, I was interested in learning how one adapts to such a grueling schedule through a 78-game season. The team had had their share of injuries, but nothing serious—just handicapping enough to keep one or two men always on the sidelines. Jarrett recovered from a separated shoulder in time for Bill White to have one. Jerry Korab's severe wrist sprain was overcome before Lou Angotti injured his ankle when one of the big boys fell on the Pest—as he is know by opposing defensemen—during a melee in front of the goal. Then Cliff Koroll took his turn at almost losing his shoulder in a separation while digging the puck out of the boards. These things plus the usual charley horses and pulled muscles provided the normal handicaps. Every team in the League had similar miseries, and no wonder—without sufficient time for the injured players to recover during the overloaded schedule.

Upon this visit to the Garden, I discovered that the press box was built as an afterthought, the architects apparently having overlooked its necessity in their plans. A sports arena without a press box is like a post office without a letter drop—and that has happened in postal planning. The omission was discovered at the time that the arena was opened and ready for business. Hastily, the back row in the mezzanine immediately under the gallery was set up to house the press corps. It was so far away from where things were going on that the local high priests of journalism wailed between the porch and the altar until officialdom set up a small and crowded space below the organist's throne where Eddie Layton reigned supreme. Two long narrow tables and twelve chairs were jammed into this pocket. Moreover, one had to descend an iron runged ladder about six feet in order to get into the pit. Executing entry is regarded as a daring feat for these sports experts, who insist upon being in the center of things but well protected. So it happened that the lords of the reportorial world nightly climbed over each other to take their assigned places in the journalistic hierarchy.

Being a visiting scribe, I was assigned a seat up in the crow's nest directly under the balcony. I shared my exile with out-of-town reporters and guests of the management. At the end of the first period of play we found our way to the pressroom for refreshment, feeling a bit leprous with rejection. The home team and the visitors rallied forces across the room from each other in the style of junior high schoolers at their first prom, although we shared the same bar. The pressroom here at the Garden, as in Detroit, was quite large and comfortably furnished with large, circular low tables and swivel armchairs. A television set was on one end of the bar so that everyone could tell when the teams were returning to the ice for the next period—a thoughtful arrangement.

Noting that the rest period was nearly over I returned to the arena, but not to my high and lofty seat. Introducing myself to the organist between "Lady of Spain" and the "Light Cavalry" theme, I visited with him for a moment as I waited for journalism's first team to file past me into their reserved section directly below.

Finally they were all in their appointed places. I had been faintly hoping that there might be a vacant chair. Nothing doing. But I did see a folding chair stuck between the back wall and small Coke cooler. So I climbed the ladder, opened the chair, and sat in the aisle.

"No spectators allowed down here, fella. This is for the press," said a reporter, a fellow with a voice like a food blender. Obviously he didn't represent *Good Housekeeping* magazine. I presented him with my press pass. "You belong up there." He motioned toward Siberia.

"I know," I answered. "I'll use this chair until someone with a prior claim comes along."

"That's a guest pass," he intoned, the fallout from his cigar wafting my way. "It's not the working press. It's just a handout from John Halligan giving you a free ride for the game."

Reaching into my jacket pocket I produced a copy of my "open sesame" letter from my editor, which by now I had come to value as a passport, and presented it to him. Before he had time to hand it back I told him to pass it along typewriter row so that everybody would know that I was not gate-crashing nor was there because I was a sportswriters'

93

fan. He made no comment, but did pass it along. Possibly at the end of the line it was dropped into the wastebasket, for it never came back to me. A more interesting contest was about to begin, anyway.

Immediately after the face-off starting the second period I felt a tap on my shoulder. Looking up I saw a late arrival. By the look in his eye I assumed that he had a squatter's right to my chair—or thought he did. So I surrendered it to him and sat on the floor at the top of the ladder.

"You're blocking the exit, Buster," came an announcement from another brother's-keeper, as insistent as a sergeant-at-arms at a lodge meeting.

"So I am," I admitted, my sap rising. "But as long as you aren't trying get down here, too, what difference does it make?" I continued to sit, but not for long. A second tardy press lord tapped me authoritatively. I moved over silently to allow his descent, wondering where he thought he was going to sit. Instead, he shared the top seat with me. When he hunkered down he spread out like a Russian weight lifter doing the clean-and-jerk. I was almost popped out of my perch. So I stood up for the remainder of the period.

Returning to the pressroom while waiting for the final period of play I still felt like a lion in a cage full of Daniels, but had a feeling that there would be some vacant seats when the game resumed. I remembered from somewhere that the press deadline for the next day's morning editions was ten P.M. The reporters in the box were typing up their accounts of the game as it went along. The game would not be over in time for the full story. However, the necessary information on the last period could be gleaned from the news service wires and the accounts filled in for the later editions. By means of acquired reportorial skills, the impression would be given that the reporters had seen the entire game. That's the way it turned out. I had a fine seat for the final period. Subsequent trips to the Garden were without incident. Apparently I had survived the journalistic version of the ordeal.

Access to the Black Hawks' dressing room was easily accomplished. In the first place they had won 5–2 over a team that was presently recovering from a series of trades. Trading always shakes up a team, especially in season, because each man wonders how secure his place is on the club. Moreover, the Rangers had been severely roughhoused and worked over in their game against the Philadelphia Flyers who were also going through the throes of trading players. The defeat by the Black Hawks followed the Flyer clash only three nights later, and the Rangers didn't seem to be back on their skates yet.

Entrance to the dressing room after a game is usually immediate and easy when the team has won and when there have not been any injuries. When there has been an injury during the game, however, and the extent of it is not known, things get tight. Naturally every reporter wants to get the complete story, which can yield comforting information to the next opponents and their coaches, so any injury that is not obvious, but possibly a handicap and a limitation on a player for a few days, is kept quiet. After the trainer and sometimes a doctor go over the injured man and give the necessary immediate treatment, he returns to the showers and dressing room and gets lost in the crowd. His condition thus remains a mystery to all outsiders. The teammates can be depended upon never to leak any information which may be of aid and comfort to their next opponent who, if they were aware of a vulnerable spot, might be tempted to work over the handicapped player. If there is delay in opening the dressing room to outsiders one suspects that something is wrong and is in the process of being covered up—a sensible procedure. When a team loses a game they are certainly in no mood to entertain visitors. Besides, after these occasions there are sometimes certain matters of conflict and misunderstanding to be straightened out, and this is always best kept within the family.

There is generally no dislike of, or aversion to, sports reporters, although there are certain specific exceptions.

The players regard these men as individuals who are trying to make a living, too, and realize that athletes are public figures. Mostly athletes and sportswriters cooperate with each other because there is a degree of mutual interdependence. The individuals who are heartily disliked are the sycophants—the brown-nosers. They are known among athletes as "jock-sniffers." They are the people who brag to their friends about athletes they have met and claim they know on an intimate basis. They can't emulate them but they use these men for their own personal identification. The jock-sniffer, by trying to associate and identify himself with sports heroes is saved from a necessity of hopelessly trying to imitate them. Simply by hanging around he hopes that the aura of stardom will rub off on him and can afterwards impress his slack-jawed friends that he, too, is super. After dealing with these characters and hangers-on it is no wonder that an athlete sometimes thinks that he exists to be taken advantage of.

Not having been with the team for a few games, I enjoyed the family reunion flavor of visiting with them for these few minutes and making plans to meet them on the morrow in Philadelphia. The usual postgame rush was on in the dressing room, for they were leaving immediately for Philadelphia. There is a League rule that requires each team to leave right away for their next game even though it may be twenty-four hours or more away. The reason is the eternal uncertainty of travel conditions, especially in flying. Buses are used for the short hauls, but the practice prevails anyway. One can understand the problems created by having 15,000 fans in a stadium and the scheduled opposing team stranded somewhere with little or no possibility of showing up. Hence the required time margin.

Doug Jarrett motioned me over to his cubicle where he was dressing. "Remember those calling cards you gave me?" he asked.

"Oh, yeah, the *un*-Christmas present," I recalled. Back around the first of December I had prepared a personal business card for each member of the team. I had a couple of dozen of them printed and enclosed in a plastic card case for each member of the Black Hawks. They read:

DOUG JARRETT

I am a very important member of
The Chicago Black Hawks.
In case of an accident, notify a
Bishop
(Preferably the S.O.B.—the
SHEPHERD OF BLACK HAWKS)

When I gave these out after they had won over St. Louis, everyone seemed pleased. ("First time I ever got anything from a fan and writer," commented Pit Martin.)

"Well, the other night I was stopped by the highway patrol for speeding," Doug said, his eyes sparkling. "When the patrolman asked for my driver's license I handed him one of those cards you gave me along with it. The cop read it, using his flashlight."

"Thank you, Mr. Jarrett, I am happy to make your acquaintance," the officer had said. "Now I want you to have my card, and with it goes an invitation to be my guest at court—and bring the Bishop along."

10

Jawboning

●

Leaving the dressing room with a "Good night, I'll see you at hotel in Philadelphia tomorrow morning," I hurried to the train station to begin my hour ride home fortified with reading material on hockey that I had picked up on my New York trip. I became interested in a study that had been done on hockey by Joe Cohen, the assistant to the vice-president of operations at Madison Square Garden. He had recently completed his master's thesis at the University of Pennsylvania's Wharton School of Finance. He was not trying to score points in sociology, but he was working toward his master's degree in marketing. Joe opened a Pandora's box of unusual and surprising opinions which are of consuming interest to the devotees of the Quartet of American Sports: baseball, basketball, football, and hockey. He has laid the foundation for someone to build on who would like to find out what kind of people prefer one sport to another, as well as the critical distance line between each sport in relation to the other three.

Over 4,000 questionnaires were submitted to fans at the Philadelphia Spectrum. This was accomplished at four of the Philadelphia Flyers hockey games and four basketball games of the Philadelphia 76ers. About 1,000 fans of each sport took the trouble to fill out the questionnaires and return them. Although this is but one small sampling in a single locality and therefore decidedly inconclusive, nevertheless the study provides some clues to the similarities and relationships of each sport to the others.

It was not too surprising to learn that nearly a third of the hockey fans in the United States admit that they don't know much about the game. Yet, an increasing number of them watch it in the arenas when seats are available— which is seldom. The television audience numbers in the millions. Except for such cities as Boston, Chicago, Detroit, and New York, where big-time hockey has been a major sport for many years so the fans there *are* knowledgeable about the game, hockey is largely regarded elsewhere as an example of vulgarian elegance and showmanship. Too many people take it for granted that hockey was born on ice —out of wedlock, the offspring of union between lacrosse and an Indian scalping raid. It is also explained away in much of the United States as having been smuggled across the border because of this nation's need, propensity, and preference for violence in sports. Some imperceptive spectators even assume that the fights and melees are planned and dramatized as they obviously are in what is wrongly called "professional wrestling." They couldn't be further from the truth.

There are ample statistics to demonstrate that ice hockey has overtaken basketball in fan attendance *and* on television. Jack Ramsay, the basketball coach of the Philadelphia 76ers and a highly competent architect of his trade, was asked for his opinions about the rise of interest in hockey and its growth in popularity as a spectator sport. He gave three reasons: first, the violence of the sport; secondly, its snob appeal; and thirdly, its color. By "color," I conclude that the perceptive Mr. Ramsay might have meant that the increasing popularity of hockey is partially due to the fact that all of its players and practically all of its spectators are white. I doubt if he meant that there was more "color" in terms of athletic drama or personalities. Hockey is the only remaining so-called "white man's" game. This is simply because there have not been a sufficient number of blacks who have had the opportunity to grow up with the sport and get in those necessary 10,000 hours of practice before becoming a pro. There are not many black spectators because there aren't any black players—yet. So far it is a sport with which they have had no experience on the playground or vacant lot as children.

The predominance of black athletes in basketball is the direct result of the opportunity that they have had to play the sport from very early childhood. I daresay there are many black boys going into their teen-age growing period who have dreams and hopes of being seven feet tall. Basketball success, like success in other sports, can be an honorable way out of poverty. When ice-skating rinks are available as basketball courts and vacant lots, we will have black hockey players.

Eldridge Cleaver comments in *Soul on Ice:* "Our mass spectator sports are geared to disguise, while affording expression to, and the acting out in elaborate pageantry of the myth of the fittest in the process of surviving." This is almost the last expression of Social Darwinism. When the blacks grow up with hockey, and excel in it, as they are likely to do in another generation, this will be another way for them to come into their own in professional sports.

Speaking of another kind of color, that of personal drama, football certainly has it. Basketball especially has it in the way that hockey does. These indoor sports are played under stressful conditions of heavy traffic on the court and rink. The spectator can see the faces of the players. He can hear the give-and-take between opponents. These sports provide a certain intimacy with the fan that baseball and even football by their nature cannot do. Lamentably, "color" has almost disappeared from baseball, it seems, since this sport, America's pastime, has become the dignified pillar and image of dull civic righteousness. This is unfortunate and sadly true. Baseball is hard put to it to come up with promotional gimmicks to fill its huge parks. At a recent Yankee bat day the management gave away 29,000 bats. This made the overhead costs for the day quite steep, but they were keeping an eye to the future by cultivating customers for the next decade. Can you imagine needing to give away hockey sticks? That would make the Grant Park riots look like a Currier and Ives print of a Sunday afternoon in Central Park, circa 1880. Likewise, there is no present promotional need for basketball or football. It is next to impossible to buy tickets for these three sports as it is.

There is a hidden danger to the long-time survival of these three sports. Basketball, football, and hockey are severing themselves from the fans. They rely on television for their popularity. Television in turn has oversaturated the armchair athlete in football, and in time will likely do the same to these other sports. Television, like poison ivy, gives the itch to whatever it touches. I hope that neither basketball nor hockey will scratch themselves to death from dermatitis of the wallet.

What is it that lies behind the appeal of these sports in our society, regardless of the form that the game takes?

Since the beginning of time, man, among other things a gregarious character, has congregated in huge crowds for special, nonpolitical occasions. I used to think that Cecil B.

De Mille's crowd scenes in his epic movies were a bit over-done. I discovered in my own studies later that he was highly accurate on his numbers. He had done his home-work, too.

There is a similarity between the days of triumphal Rome and our day. Among other things, the Romans also experienced a population explosion. Furthermore, their in-terest in competitive sports, which were considerably more bloody than ours, is evident in the size and number of their stadia and arenas. It is estimated that the Colosseum in Rome held over 80,000 spectators *every day* during the sea-son. The Circus Maximus could hold three times that num-ber. The same was true of contest places throughout the Empire. Today's announcers proclaim in cathedral tones that the arena is packed (15,000), or that the stadium has a capacity crowd (80,000), for the Big Game. Apparently we have a long way to go.

In a nonsports oriented culture, such as Asia in general and India in particular, it is not uncommon to have gather-ings of a nonpolitical nature in excess of three million peo-ple. Why do people gather together in such incredible num-bers? It is hard to explain to us Westerners. *Darshan* is the experience of being in a huge crowd. It is a form of happi-ness induced by Hindu people through being in the presence of some great manifestation of their collective unconscious. It sets up a glow of suprapersonal joy. It has with it a bless-ing or benediction, but not in the ordinary theological or ecclesiastical sense of the word, since it is not bestowed or conferred. It "happens."

There is a stir of common joy in Eastern *darshan.* I think we have a Western version that we experience when we are in our relatively smaller crowds (Remember, I am speaking of *non*-political gatherings. It seems to me that these kinds of meetings induce a "pseudo-*darshan*" except in the case of the drawing power of an obviously charis-matic person. We may try to dispose of the implications of *darshan* by calling it "crowd spirit," "game pageantry," "the team is up," but these terms are all pathetically inadequate to explain what goes on in the hearts of players and spectators, and perhaps watchers on television as well. Now, with the advent of television, we are being made witnesses, and *not* participants, in *darshan.* The impersonality takes half the joy out of it.

As I have already suggested, the American fan is drawn to sports contests as iron filings to a magnet because he finds order there. He finds precision, skill, logical steps, pattern, and *achievement of purpose.* He can retire from his messed-up and confused personal life into a situation that has a solution. He can watch his representative on the court or field or rink fulfill purpose and do it gracefully. He can see men who know what they are doing. This is a Western form of *darshan,* the stir of common joy.

Getting down to the basic elements of each sport aside from the charactersitics defined above, let's note first *comparative* differences. The first is speed. The second is the collision factor. The order—from fast to slow—is hockey, football, basketball, and baseball. The speed-collision factor is called "violence" in football and hockey. In basketball it is "competition under the boards for ball-control." In baseball it is either "The bum didn't see me coming in" or "That clown blocked the baseline." These are usually called a "one-to-one relationship," as sociologists and psychologists are fond of calling conflicts, from the classroom or the grandstand. This kind of togetherness reaches a peak in hockey, football, basketball, and baseball—in that order— because it is in direct proportion to the speed of the colliding players.

Basketball, being played on a smaller field compared to other major sports, has a much heavier traffic pattern. A lot of fender-bending goes on under the basket. But the player's mph factor is not as great as in football or hockey. The resemblance of hockey to a stock-car demolition race certainly gives it a more spectacular characteristic. In football, to use a similar though ungraceful analogy, you have huge, beautifully coordinated bodies moving at a speed that seems to compare with a semitrailer truck on an expressway. There is only one thing for you or me to do if we want to survive. Pull over to the side and watch the trucks compete among themselves for cruising space. Now, the hockey player is on a motorcycle on this freeway-arena. He gets around faster, wearing those knives on his feet and waving a decapitator about. The inevitable collision is bound to be more spectacular and exciting. It is also conducive to instant retaliation. (This is a "restraint" word that means "fisticuffs.") In football the offended and violated player waits for the next play from scrimmage to pop his man. In basketball he bides his time until the opposition has the ball. Present judgment is meted out under the boards. In baseball, if you don't get on base again in that game, you have to wait until the next day or the next series or the next season. By that time the fan has been diverted to other indelicate scenes and has probably forgotten all about it, whether the players have or not.

There is another reason for the popularity of ice hockey. There are no times-out. There are three 20-minute periods of carefully organized mayhem as the teams act out the chasing of a fire engine going the wrong way on a one-way street. There is no pause factor in hockey except for the face-offs and the occasional fisticuffs when time stops and the confusion begins.

When things go wrong in basketball or football and a breather is desired, a time-out may be called, up to a certain limit of them per period. There are official times-out for the referees. And in all but hockey there is the pause between plays while players are picking up the fragments of themselves. In football there is a fifteen-minute total of elapsed time in scrimmage action. And that is an extremely strenuous few seconds on each play. In basketball it runs to forty-eight minutes, with times-out allowed. In hockey, except for the break every twenty minutes, the spectator receives almost a full 60-minute hour of action.

11

The Industry

●

The following morning I managed to get to downtown Philadelphia and the Penn Center Inn, where the Black Hawks
stayed the previous night, in time for breakfast with Dennis
Hull. Ever since he had told me about skating the fourteen-
mile round trip in order to find some boys to play hockey
with, I wanted to talk to him more.

"Dennis," I began, "I've been wondering for some time
exactly how you break into hockey. How were you 'discovered,' if I may use the word, in a tiny company town on
Quinney Bay?"

"That's easy. All the towns in Canada having any size at all sponsor Junior Hockey. It's a community project, like your Little League baseball. The local Service Clubs buy the uniforms and pay for the team's ice time. The boys are classified according to age."

"How far were you from one of these towns? Were you in Little League, as we call it?"

"We went to town and signed up for Junior Hockey. All you have to have is a certificate of birth or something legal that states your age and birthday. And you have to have your own skates, of course. Then you're assigned to a team and begin to play hockey according to the rules. No more 'shinty.'"

"That's still for removed from big-time hockey," I remarked. "What's the next step?"

"You advance up through the leagues through high school. Scouts from the National Hockey League make their rounds, and when they see someone who looks as though he might develop, they talk to you and your folks about trying out for what's called 'Junior *A* Hockey League.'"

"Was he seeking you out because you were Bobby's brother?" I asked, tentatively.

"I don't think so. Scouts get to watch every Canadian hockey player sooner or later, anyway. But the talent scout was from the Black Hawks system. He was recruiting for tryouts for St. Catherine's Junior *A* Black Hawks and, of course, he did find Bobby the same way about five years before I came along.

"Any boy who has the talent and ability in hockey is given every opportunity to find out if he has enough going for him to make the NHL. It's every Canadian boy's dream. We all take it pretty seriously."

"During these Junior League days did you get much coaching?"

"About the same as in your Little League baseball," he explained. "You get more advice than good instruction, and then only on game days when, as a team, you have ice time.

I think that parents are a big factor. My Dad has always skated. He'd watch us boys out on the bay, and when he'd see us doing something wrong, he'd correct us right then."

"Not only in skating, but in learning how to handle a stick and move a puck, and everything, I suppose."

"Right," agreed Dennis. "You've got to learn these things early before you develop a lot of bad habits. If you don't correct those early in the game, then your talent and ability can't be put to work for you."

Doug Jarrett came in and joined us.

"You know," continued Dennis, "I can tell the players on the ice whose parents got them started right. Some of the men have talent and ability but they weren't trained in basics, and their play shows it."

"Then there are those guys who make it in the NHL for a while on sheer aggressiveness but never really learned the game as kids," added Jarrett.

"Yeah," said Dennis, "and then there are those guys without talent whose only ability is skating up the other guy's back. You know, the roughhouser."

"He does all he can, "Doug smiled, "but there aren't very many of them who can hold up under the season schedule, year in and year out. And besides that, I do everything I can to discourage them, including my 190 pounds."

We heard a loud complaint from the next table. Lou Vargas, equipment man, was cussing his bad luck and informing Jim Pappin at the same time that his gear bag was missing. "It was on the cart from the dressing room to the pick-up truck. Between there and the bus some guy swiped it, that's what," he explained. "it's a wonder they didn't steal the truck." Pappin just looked at Lou and shook his head as he sat down.

"At least being with the Black Hawks will make a philosopher out of you," I joked.

"Philosopher, hell! A madman's more like it. Now why in the hell would anybody steal a hockey suit?" Lou roared.

"To sell the skates and the stick for a 'fix,' " I suggested.

Ignoring the explanation, Lou fell to mumbling about getting another outfit for Jim in time for the game that night. Jerry Korab, the new 215-pound defenseman, turned to me and said, "When do I get my calling cards?"

I didn't know if he was kidding or not but I said, "That's right. You joined the team a week afterward, didn't you? O.K. I'll have a set made for you and send them on."

"They won't work on cops," testified Jarrett. "I oughta know."

A quorum of Black Hawks were in the dining room. In spite of the predominance of young men, the customers didn't seem to be aware of who they were. Not being football or basketball athletes, they were not eye-stopping in size. Even the larger ones, such as Korab, Bill White, or Eric Nesterenko weren't over 6'2". Giantism hasn't hit hockey yet, although scouts and coaches are looking for big men. Hockey's idea of bigness, though, is the size of these afore-mentioned men. There's a limit as to how far one can go on skates in combining size and speed.

There was considerable shifting around between tables. Some arrived, others left. Some were reading the newspapers, and the rest of us talked quietly, now that Lou had done his ventilating. Cliff Koroll was sitting next to me now, so I asked him how he came to the Black Hawks, after graduating from Denver University.

"I take it," I started, "that you didn't play in the Junior A hockey."

"That's right," agreed Cliff. "I had always wanted to go to college. The hockey coach from Denver was up in Saskatoon, where I lived and asked me about going to college and playing hockey. That was exactly what I wanted. Call me lucky, I guess." Koroll is a rather handsome and intense young man, a quiet and yet apparently a relaxed sort of person; he has a curious turn of mind and is interested in everything and everyone about him.

"You made All-American in collegiate hockey, didn't you?" I asked.

"Oh yes. That's how I got my tryout with the Black Hawks. I found out right away that I needed a year's experience in professional hockey before I would be ready for the National Hockey League. I played my first year with Dallas and then came up to the Black Hawks."

"And what a start with the Black Hawks," I said. "Eighteen goals and nineteen assists as a rookie that first year."

"You know," Cliff said, "I don't know what it's like to play on a losing team. We won all through college. I was always with a winner in Junior Hockey. I don't see how some of these men can play game after game with a losing club. I don't know if I could do it or not."

I reminded Cliff that when he started with the Black Hawks they floundered around in last place all through the fall of 1969.

"That's right," he agreed, "but we got hold of ourselves and went on to the division championship."

"Yeah," I said, "but you *almost* had your chance."

"All the same, I know I wouldn't like it. I *do* know that it would affect my play, perhaps permanently. That happens to some fine players, you know."

As we sat there talking I noticed that the four at our table were all college graduates and made the observation. "How many are there on the squad?" I asked.

"If you mean the ones with degrees," volunteered Gerry Pinder, "there must be seven or eight. There are some like me who are working toward degrees in the off-season."

"The number is increasing," I said, running my memory-scanner back and forth over the books on hockey that I had read preparatory to this assignment.

"I've been predicting for the last four or five years that within ten years—even in Canada—most professional players will be coming out of the colleges," remarked Pit Martin. "The Junior Hockey programs are not going to be as important a source of players."

"Why is that?" I asked.

"Because you can't play hockey at this level of compe-

109

tence all your life," he answered. "I do quite a bit of public speaking around Chicago," he added, "and whenever I speak to kids I tell them that they may be pretty good hockey players, or think they are, but that's not enough. You're going to have to hack it with the books if you're going to get anywhere in life. Without an education it's back to the mines with the lunch bucket, and that's hard to do after a few years in National League Hockey."

"What about athletic scholarships for promising players?" I asked Pit.

"Colleges are being forced to cut back on them. I think the emphasis is turning toward good hockey players who are also good students."

"How did it go with you?" I asked him.

"I went three years to McMaster University in Hamilton while I was playing Junior *A*. I finished in the summer schools."

"With what?"

"A degree in history. But I was lucky because I had parents who had enough confidence in me to trust that I wouldn't waste time around pool halls. I found there was plenty of time to do my studying and play hockey, even with a 50-game schedule."

"Many potentially good hockey players never get beyond Junior Hockey," put in Koroll. "There is a reluctance on the part of a lot of parents to let their sons go into the game. The junior clubs have earned a bad reputation because 60 to 70 percent of the players drop out of school."

"Yeah," interposed Pit, "what happens is that the boys do pretty well at hockey and they hear how good they are and then they start believing it. They say to themselves, "Why should I bother with schoolwork? I'll be a professional player." What they don't realize is that only 3 percent of the kids in junior hockey ever make it to the big league."

"The same situation exists percentage-wise here in the States," added Magnuson. "How many college players ever make it into pro football? For that matter, how many American athletes make it to the big leagues in football or basketball?"

"Baseball seems to be the only exception," I agreed, "and even in that sport there are more and more college grads or men with some kind of specialized training."

I began recalling small-town semipro sports when I was a boy. I remembered them chiefly for being a collection of the local toughs from around the county who never practiced together but teamed up on Sunday to battle the visiting bullies from other towns the same size. Dirty Dalton was imported from 50 miles away to play quarterback for the American Legion football team. He scorned both helmet and shoulder pads. We kids watched him recover during the half by knocking off a quart of home brew down at the far end of the field. " 'Goats' Doig was another of that fraternity," I went on.

"There are still those kind of characters in Canadian hockey in small towns," reflected Cliff. "I think they *all* used to be that way in the early days of pro hockey."

"I was reading in one of the books on the history of hockey about the team from the Yukon that challenged Montreal, the Stanley Cup champions back around the turn of the century," I said. "The only practice they had for the game was in a baggage car on the five-day rail trip."

"Yeah," said Pit, "and they were beaten 17–0, too."

"Speaking of beatings, you fellows know what the Flyers did to the New York Rangers the other night, don't you?" mentioned Mag.

"They beat 'em 5–2," answered Martin.

"I was there," I said. "But they didn't beat them playing hockey. They bullied them all over the ice and pushed them around in that first period. The Rangers never knew what hit them. Nobody got around to playing hockey until the second period, and by then it was too late."

"I'm not surprised," said Magnuson. "There's been a lot of trading going on there. Everybody gets upset."

"Maggie, your favorite boxing opponent, Heiskala, was

111

traded to San Diego, wasn't he?" kidded Pit, who's generally a serious person (and reputed to be the fastest skater in the NHL by many). "Got a new victim picked out?"

I broke in again because I cannot resist coaching. "Just watch those guys tonight, that's all." I counseled.

They smiled paternally on me as we broke up the meeting. Some were going to the movies, some to wander, and I to a brief appointment elsewhere downtown. I did not see them again until game time.

My uneasy feelings about the Flyer game were justified. The game was scarcely two minutes old when a Finnish hockey player by the name of Earl slammed Keith Magnuson into the boards with a brutal smash. Magnuson was understandably surprised because the puck was 60 feet away at the time, and he was minding his own business, not realizing the impending doom. He had no chance to avoid the collision nor to protect himself from it. It was one, two, three—crash-bang—and that was it.

As Magnuson slowly got to his feet, and it could be seen that his legs were behaving independently of each other and sort of dangling from his waist while tentatively supporting his body, he skated about in a small circle, shaking his head and trying to refocus his eyes. Bill White skated out to be the relief man. Mag couldn't find the bench but he knew dimly that he was supposed to get off the ice.

"Hey, Mag! Over here! We're over here!" Somebody whistled at him. He followed the sound and eventually stumbled into the bench and sat down, staring blankly straight ahead, trying to put his fragmented self together.

During this time while Bill White was spelling Keith, Earl the Finn was serving time in the penalty box for you-know-what. A third defense line went into play, so White didn't have a chance to discuss the matter with Earl, who was still in the penalty box. Now Pat Stapleton and Doug Jarrett skated to the defense positions. Earl came back on the ice. He received an early treatment.

The game went into the second period before Keith and Earl were on the ice at the same time. Mag's eyes were focusing again, and he beaded them on Earl and took off down the ice. The last words I heard were: "I'm skating up that guy's back and chase him clear out of the League." It cost Mag two minutes in the penalty box, but Earl didn't play any more that night. A couple of weeks later I read that he had been traded down. *Sic transit gloria* hockey player-fighter.

Bobby Hull spends very little time in the penalty box, but on this night he had been followed and pestered by a player who was assigned to stay on Hull's back but not to try to get the puck away from him. The strategy apparently was to distract Bobby sufficiently so that a stick artist could move in and steal the puck. It makes the story better if the reader knows that the appointed nuisance was still recovering from oral surgery. He had struggled thus far through most of the season never being free from jaw and dental pain. When Hull could no longer tolerate his tormentor he swung his stick at him just below waist-high and caught the gadfly solidly in the groin, and down he went. As Bobby returned to the bench after serving his penalty, he observed that for the first time in two months Herb's jaw didn't hurt.

Throughout the game, the Flyers slammed and bullied their way through a team that had come to play hockey. By the end of the second period, they led 4–1, and each team scored once in the last period to make the final score 5–2. There were some bruised-up boys in the dressing room that night and nobody had anything much to say.

I went up to Stan Mikita. "Double-dose your vitamins tonight, Stan," I said consolingly. This was an in-joke which dated back at the first of the season.

Having flown into Chicago for the game with Vancouver, I had no way to my host's home after the game. I knew that Stan lived in the same suburb, so I asked him if I could bum a ride out with him. After we got in the car and started out he remarked that he was going to be stiff and sore in the morning.

"I feel it more this year than ever before," he said. "It shouldn't be age, though—I'll be thirty-one this year."

"Ever try natural vitamins and wheat germ?" I asked.

"Are you a food nut?" Stan asked directly.

"No, I'm not," I answered, "but I stay away from as many synthetic foods as possible." I went on to explain my ideas that had grown out of experimenting and how I found a nutrition supplement that made me well and keeps me well.

"How can I find out about it?" he asked.

"I'll be downtown tomorrow and I'll find a paperback that makes sense on the subject of nutrition."

"That'll be great," Stan enthused. "I'll be waiting."

Monday and Tuesday went by before I saw Stan to talk with. We were both at workouts but he was being followed around by some fellow with a proposition that would make Stan a millionaire (he said). So it was Wednesday of the game before I gave Stan the paperback that I had bought. I also got some natural vitamins and wheat germ for him and left the package in his cubicle. That night he got four goals and an assist. Stan simply couldn't miss the net that night.

After the game I came tearing down to the dressing room and called out, "What did you do, Stan? Take both bottles?"

"They're right here in the sack on the bench where you left 'em," he grinned.

"Well," I said, a little disappointed, "that goes to show you that you'd better go easy with that stuff. Look what happened when the charm was put in your cubicle." We both laughed.

As Stan headed for the shower I peeked in the bag. The seal was broken on the vitamin bottle.

Some years ago I was sitting in a stadium with a professor of English and waiting for the football game to begin. We were watching 60 men warming up for the game.

"Just think," he philosophized. "This school could put on Shakespeare's plays for a year on the money that is spent on jockstraps alone."

I reminded him that even so, probably half his salary was paid out of the profits of the athletic department. With the present crisis in education on college campuses, even Notre Dame University has ended its opposition to postseason bowl games. The money received, declared their President, Fr. Theodore Hessburgh, would help tremendously in maintaining educational standards. For many, this is enough to make strong men weep, but think upon how much big-time athletics has done for academia.

In the relentless march of sports evolution it was inevitable that professional sports would be the end product, the apotheosis of athletic competition. Professional baseball arrived at its present popularity largely without drawing players from college ranks. Football and basketball franchises choose their personnel entirely from the ranks of college athletes. In NHL player selection, most of the men come to the big time through the farm system, usually upon completion of high school. Only quite recently has scouting and recruitment of collegiate hockey begun.

This has become a necessary part of the scene because of the growing and unceasing demand for athletes who are experts in the art of executing that which is difficult. The outcome of a game today seldom affects the whole community as it did in the days of Casey and Mudville. A remnant of that kind of loyalty is found only in fan clubs. For nearly everyone else, The Game is an exhibition of a highly developed art form, in a certain sense, admirably performed. The ancient doctrine of the remnant, as expressed in Scripture, still lives on in a fan club. So, too, does the expectation of a messiah—a superstar who shall lead the faithful from the cellar to the heights, the playoffs, and perhaps in hockey, even the Stanley Cup, the Holy Grail of the Canadian sport. It's a long way from the icehouse to the White House.

Baseball first, followed by football, basketball, and now

hockey have emerged into a classicized form, a ritualized series of movements as crystalized as the medieval Liturgy, a Solemn High Mass conducted by athletic dignitaries. Even the spectator-congregations crammed into stadia and arenas have ritualized anger as well as ceremonial approval. Humor is as out of place here as it is in a Eucharistic Congress. Every cow of custom has become sacred.

The Game used to unite us in the feeling that we were still in high school, and planning on going to the Prom that night—if the team won. Under those circumstances, of course, the hero of the game would receive a kiss from the Prom Queen for every point that he scored during combat. All that is part of the past now, even in high school. Today loyalty to a team evaporates quickly if the team does not win. Today the stands are full when a winner is in town, but there is little else in the stands but empty cartons and blowing newspapers when the team is losing. Vince Lombardi, recently elevated to the List of Sport Saints, spoke for all modern America when he said, "Winning isn't the main thing, it is the *only* thing." Heroism, sacrifice, and suffering do not have any meaning if The Game is lost. Overnight, the losers become bums.

Among major sports only hockey retains the old mystique. Loyalties to local teams are still strong and individually marked. The game has not yet emerged into classic play formations, nor is it likely to do so. The speed factor makes the ritualizing of movement and pattern almost impossible. This sport alone has not become an exercise into order that has characterized other major sports. In watching baseball, football, or basketball in person or on television, the spectator as well as the player anticipate the next play. This is not true in hockey. Only in this game are the plays ad-libbed.

There are natural hindrances in hockey which work against its becoming stylized. The aforementioned speed of the game and its collision factor keep both teams constantly on the defensive and offensive at the same time. Furthermore, the odds are against the team that is advancing the puck. The scoring possibility, although always imminent, is less than in any other sport.

It is difficult to adapt hockey to the ways and concepts of big-time sports. The industry, as it is sometimes irreverently called, wants and needs as large an audience on television as possible, for sound economic reasons. This gives them new markets for League-endorsed products. Selling television time on hockey is difficult because there are not long nor frequent enough pauses in the game to insert the conventional commercial. When television tried to use those commercials that run over 60 seconds, there was a bad reaction from the fans. The advertisers had to be convinced that they could get an effective message across in less than 60 seconds.

The next time you watch a hockey game on television, notice how the end of the carefully timed commercial usually comes out even with the resumption of play. Occasionally this is missed by a few seconds, and the announcer must catch the viewer up on what happened during the ad. Both advertiser and announcer anxiously hope that a goal will not have been scored during the interim—or a major brawl started. There is no wrath, including a woman's scorn, that can match the anger of the fan who has missed out on a piece of action because of a sales pitch.

The answer may lie in the officials' having small receiving sets under their shirts. Then when they hear a beep they would know that the commercial is over and that play may be resumed. This would be a tricky business because it would be imprudent for the official and especially unfair to a team that has momentum going. In this regard the official would be taking on a player's role. Oftentimes one will notice during a face-off that a team that has been on the defensive much of the time will stall and lag in coming to their assigned positions around the face-off circle. This is a stratagem to slow up the opponent's momentum. Sooner or later someone will find an official way to make a buck during this pause, but it should not be at the expense of the game itself.

117

Athletic events are becoming more and more spectacular as entertainment. The ultimate criterion of the value of a sport has become its usefulness to television. The medium has had to make many adjustments and refinements in its techniques, such as instant replay, dual scenes, close-ups, and the like—and has done them well. In seeking the entertainment dollar which is now derived mostly from advertising on nationwide telecasts, it is only to be expected that each sport will also have to make certain adaptations and accommodations. The best example of this is found in the speeding up of each game. This has necessitated platoon systems and line changes in order to maintain the terrific pace. Baseball, alone, remains the only major sport that maintains its leisurely pace of early prewar America.

The development of these sports were, in their earlier stages, athletic dramatizations of Darwin's theory of natural selection. "If we do not like the survival of the fittest we have only one alternative and that is the survival of the unfittest. The former is the law of civilization. The latter is the law of un-civilization." So it was written by a Professor Sumner at Yale University in the early 1890's. It became the social philosophy of sport under Walter Camp, the father of American football, who made it into a creed and a faith of which Lombardi was the most recent prophet.

The precept of natural selection has endured until the present day although cracks in the castle walls are beginning to show with the defections from sports of men like Jim Bouton, Johnny Sample, and Dave Meggyesy, among others. They are generally regarded as envenomed victims of a remorseless Darwinian process. The argument used is that no one revolts until he discovers that he could not succeed in his game. It has never been suggested, in defense, that the real reason for defection might be that not only has the fun and pleasure gone out of the game, but furthermore the odds are too great against the player's survival in the sport that his disinterest overcomes and surpasses his talent, which he knows is being exploited and manipulated.

The Industry

While watching Jerry Kramer, formerly of the Green Bay Packers, and Dave Meggyesy on David Frost's television show, "Viewpoint," I witnessed the defense of the ancient orthodoxy of Darwin's theory. Kramer did an able and eloquent defense of the direction in which big-time sports has gone. Meggyesy came out of the confrontation labeled an apostate, if not a heretic. The judgment of the audience, determined by the applause for Kramer, gave ample evidence that the American public is still hooked on nineteenth-century science and the adaptation of sports to this theory of survival.

An interesting commentary on this is provided by Bobby Hull's remark, after he had been so harassed by Bryan Watson that Bobby struck him down on the ice. "I feel badly about it. It's not my nature to do this. Sometimes I hate this game because of the way it *changes* a man."

The attitude among athletes toward professional sports is to get what they can out of it by the use and exploitation of their talent and getting the hell out of it while they are still in one piece, hopefully financed to become their own bosses. The professional athlete is fast losing any illusions that he might have about management. He is also learning that talent and competency in athletics do not necessarily mean that he will excel at everything else. Player's agents, business advisers, and managers have become a part of the scene. In this way the player finds that he can exploit his own talent and fame as well, just as sports management has been able to do for its own profit.

Many men of big business, highly gifted, acquisitive, and hypermanic in their way regard the activities of men as survival tactics in the jungle of life. They themselves excel at pressuring and manipulating people and situations in their world. Even their recreation must involve money-risk. Witness the personal "friendly" bets in golf matches. See how this is extended in the tournament when the word is given that if a certain pro sinks his next shot, he will get a thousand bucks. Apparently they find it irresistible to watch the other fellow work under severe pressure. Only by having money involved in an activity does the action make sense. The athlete is involved in it purely by the nature of his livelihood.

Curiously enough, professional athletes on the whole are not as aggressive or competitive outside their particular arenas as they are in it. Only on the playing field does the gladiatorial spirit of survival and supremacy take precedence over everything else. But the monkey on the back of the big-time businessman never allows him to relax. Time after time the athlete proves himself the better man and probably secretly hates his management superior for what he is doing to him, to the game, and to life.

Dennis Hull

Gerry Desjardins

Eric Nesterenko

Keith Magnuson

Pit Martin

Lou Angotti

Pat Stapleton

Bill White

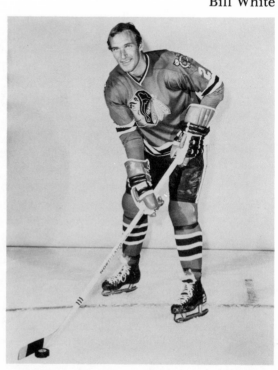

Bryan Campbell

Dan Maloney

Doug Mohns

Paul Shmyr

Gerry Pinder

Jim Pappin

"Where there's music there can't be mischief" (Cervantes, *Don Quixote*). Organist Al Melgard (*right*) and a friendly S.O.B. (Shepherd of the Black Hawks).

12

"Thou Shalt Not Back Down"

●

"Mebbe we did lose that game, but we won the fight," is the frequent comment of an old-timer when he reminisces about the good old days. Now that hockey has come of age as a national sport, people ask if fights are an integral part of the game or are staged. Oftener than not, this is the first question that comes up. Some persons ask if the fights can be eliminated. Then comes the question behind the question: does the National Hockey League *want* to eliminate them?

My reply is that fights are an inescapable part of hockey. Whether by accident or by game plan, they exist at all levels of the game. Some battles result from a melee and simply escalate into a first-rate skirmish. Other fights have been brewing for weeks, usually from the time the teams last met. Other fights happen when a team is being outplayed and somebody decides to win by intimidating and outslugging the other team.

The tension is unrelievedly high throughout the game on both ice and bench. The players are constantly and totally "involved." When they're not engaged on the ice, they may well be continuing the battle verbally from the bench —and with as much gusto. On the bench, the bodies may rest but "effort" goes on.

One has to be down among them to get the full flavor of the players' heckling of each other. Occasionally a television camera sweep lets us see their lips move, their heads shake, their faces turn a smile or a frown. Sometimes we can detect some advice shouted to an official or a recommendation as to where he should go at once and what he should do when he gets there. Opposing players, of course, also receive such suggestions. At various times I have been within range of fragments of conversations on the bench, hearing the comments that a player will make about an opponent as he comes off the ice and gets his breath back—and also verbal spears shot into the rink to let an opponent know that all is not forgiven.

Here are some sallies and exchange of Hawk-talk from the bench in the heat of various battles. Not surprisingly, they can be a little gamy:

"Hey, you guys, watch out for Pierre. He's skating his ass off tonight. Must'a got wind that he's gonna be sent down."

"Watch Alexis! He's stick-swinging like a peasant woman flailing wheat. I damn near got decapitated."
"De-what?"
"Get your ass chopped off with a stick, stupid."

Defenseman coming off the ice during a particularly

rough game: "Another game like this and it's back to the mine and the lunch bucket for me. That bastard's meaner than my old lady."

"I don't see what's so special about René. When he was skating for the Maple Leafs you could always get into the stadium."

"What's got into Dave? He skates like he had a hot hockey puck up his ass."
"Yeah. Either that or he's got his jockstrap on backwards."

"Hey, look who's coming out on the ice! Did your wife let you out tonight, Bugsy?"
"Yeah. Look at him. There goes the neighborhood."

"Hey, Fizz, who's your skating teacher? Peggy Fleming? Stay over. The Ice Follies comes in tomorrow night and you can earn an honest living."

"Giorgio thinks grapenuts is a disease."

"C'mon you guys! Let's get the puck out'a here!"

"Look at Jean eating pucks tonight. I'm all in tryin' to slam hot ones past him and he swallows 'em all. Balls!"

Of course, there are also other kinds of continuous conversation, such as plans on how to break up a certain offensive line or an observation by a player on the bench to a skating teammate about how the latter is being played by his opponent, plus a suggestion as to what he might do about it. It is not all heckling. In fact, when a team is in a scoring slump and each offensive line, which is supposed to do the scoring, knows exactly how long it has been since they racked up a goal, there isn't much conversation by those unlucky fellows. They have eyes for nobody but the statistician. Defensive lines who are on the ice too often when goals are scored against them suffer the same anxieties. In both cases the players may be quiet, but they are still under tension made keener by their sense of frustration.

Given such anger and agony and sheer competitiveness, it would be asking too much of any group of men who are constantly in collision always to behave themselves with perfect decorum. Under these circumstances the impressive thing, to my mind, is not that fights happen but that they happen comparatively seldom.

When they happen, however, they are for real. Because the players are on ice and are awkward without their sticks, the scraps might look comical and perhaps fakey at times, but there's nothing funny about the punches that land, as any hockey player will tell you.

The National Hockey League does not encourage fighting. It doesn't have to because there are always enough players willing to use their fists at the slightest invitation. "I'm not going to condemn my players for fighting," said Coach Billy Reay. "That's what they're supposed to do when challenged, or they'd be run out of the League."

Purist fans may dislike the brawls, as do a large number of the players. But coaches and players both know that there is *no* way to avoid them and remain competitive. So, the NHL is not about to attempt to curtail the battling. The player who really wants revenge might choose to get it during a scramble by applying a stick to his tormentor's throat when the chances are good that he won't get caught. He may sometimes wait until the next time the teams play, and after having balanced the personal score, skate away to the penalty box with a grim smile on his face as the vanquished victim picks himself up off the ice and begins to remember that the reason for the attack was the agenda which remained incomplete from the last time he and his attacker met.

Because fans love fights, on the whole, does not mean that the fights are staged or encouraged. They are merely allowed to develop naturally. To understand this from a fan's point of view, remember that after a hard day's work, or even more so, if it has been a week since he has watched a game, it is pure joy for a spectator to see someone strike back at injustice and mete out present judgment. During that magic moment the fan *is* the player on the ice.

Much of the roughness remains in the game because it is part of the very essence of this first of collision sports in which the impact speed is normally about 40 miles an hour. And not only the speed makes the game exciting and tension-filled. We have already discussed developments in the game that have keyed up the action. Changes of the rules in recent years have converted the rinks into shooting galleries in which goalies ever more frequently have to ward off slap shots and must try to deal with brutal screen plays. The curved stick blade makes shots on goal even more deadly. Small wonder that face masks have mercifully been devised for goalies and that there is no longer any dishonor felt in wearing them. Similarly, more players are feeling the wisdom of wearing helmets. Each concussion gains a convert, it is said.

The aim of the game, however, is not to maim. Hockey is neither as barbaric nor as simple as that. The idea is still to put the puck in the other team's net. While it is true that he is going to get in your way and obstruct you in every way that he can, hoping the referee isn't looking, the attacking player must outflank the enemy and at high speed overcome all obstacles.

In *Look* Magazine ice hockey was portrayed as a vicious sport especially designed to encourage cruelty, mayhem, and sudden death—after the appropriate shedding of one's own blood in front of 15,000 people. The article implied that hockey players are regarded as possessing a combination of the finest animal traits and the poorest human traits. The writer gave the impression that hockey players are poison-fanged monsters whose great joy in life is to split heads and revel in blood lust.

This is manifestly unfair, dishonest, and untrue. Fighting and stick-swinging exile one to the penalty box. Enough of it can lose games and end careers. Bobby Hull holds a dim view of slashing and fighting: "The team that does these things sits out its own destruction in the penalty box."

The misleading *Look* article displayed a large picture of Hull bleeding profusely from a cut across the nose, obviously inflicted by a hockey stick. Most of the time, such a blow is accidental. You wouldn't have any way of knowing this except that players admit it when asked. Many times such an injury happens when a teammate skates toward a player at the moment of a backswing preceding a slap shot —occasionally by his own buddy whom he did not suspect was about to take a shot on goal. The results are the same. This particular picture of Bobby in his sufferings also shows the restraining arm of the referee apparently separating him from his tormentor. The implication from the picture and the accompanying words under it was that Hull is a monster who had been stopped by a brave David. Ergo, the greater the star, the greater the capacity for destroying his opposition. Implied lies. All of it.

There are two sports in which the object is to maim or incapacitate the opponent. These are boxing and wrestling, in their various Western and Oriental forms. Football is becoming this sort of game in our day, although all major sports, in their strategy, seek to keep certain opponents out of a particular play. The aim of the offense, of course, is to score. But a large part of the strategy which leads to this is the blocking out and inconveniencing the opponent obstacle. When an opponent finds himself energetically unwelcome and he has been suddenly rendered powerless, he will naturally try to nullify the attempt of his opponent to put him out of the play. He isn't particularly interested in taking him out of the contest or out for the rest of the season, nor is he interested in destroying an opponent's career. Alas, this cannot be said to hold true always in professional football although fewer athletes than one might think ever engage in administering real damage.

The so-called badmen of sport are few in number and

are made up mostly of those players who try to compensate for lesser talent by roughhousing and bullying any opponent in sight. This appeals to that segment of fans who live the same way in their own lives—or would like to if they had the courage. The same conditions prevail in hockey. The superstars, the stars, and other most effective players in hockey spend the least amount of time in the penalty box. A look at the *Hockey Guide Annual* shows quite clearly that the bullies of the world's fastest sport rank highest in penalty minutes and lowest in scoring and assists.

Stan Mikita tells how he used to take on any and all comers at the slightest provocation when he began his career with the Black Hawks. In his book *I Play to Win,* he relates that he came home after a game and was met by his very young daughter who asked why Daddy was sitting all alone on a bench so much when the team was losing and why didn't he go out on the ice and help them win. The moment of truth hit Stan suddenly. He realized that he had so much talent that there wasn't really any point in suggesting a lack of it by sitting in a penalty box. He concluded that serving time is not a good way to demonstrate ability—unless unnecessary roughness is all that one has to contribute to the sport.

As you watch hockey you will soon begin to see that the team bully, or "policeman," as he is sometimes called, seldom takes on the supertalented players. In the first meeting of the 1970–71 season between the New York Rangers and the Black Hawks a Ranger rookie, Syl Apps, Jr. the son of Syl Apps of Hall of Fame renown, fouled Bobby Hull in a way that Bobby considered unnecessary and purposeless. Now Hull is one of the ablest and most competitive as well as noncombative players in the League. This night Apps worked over Hull who suddenly and unexpectedly retaliated. Bobby turned on Syl beat him to the ice in a storm of fists, gathered up his poise and dignity and skated slowly to the penalty box for a ten-minute penance—his only penalty all season. Apps received two minutes for high-sticking, ten

127

minutes for fighting, and the congratulations of the Rangers and the New York crowd for arranging to keep Hull out of the game for a spell. Depending upon whose side one is on, I suppose that this could be regarded as a case of vicarious sacrifice on Apps's part. As it turned out, however, this brave nonsense brought forth nothing. The Rangers could not score even though the Black Hawks had Hull off the ice.

Immediately after the game, as the teams were returning to their dressing rooms, Bobby skated up to Syl and apologized to him while at the same time giving him some veteran's advice not to try that stuff on old-timers because a next time *might* jeopardize his career. Bobby quietly made it clear that any more of those tactics repeated on him would mean that the perpetrator would have to be peeled off the boards with a putty knife. Men like Hull and Mikita aren't bothered overmuch by bully rookies who are trying to establish status and recognition for themselves by incapacitating stars. The philosophy among the talented is to let the lesser talented rookies knock each other off.

The game's roughhousers, as a rule, do not have very long careers in the League. They wear out faster and become even less effective because of continuous injuries received in their compensating tactics. One finds very few unintelligent men in professional athletics. What few there are will be found among the bullies. If I shave down the meaning and give even the bully the benefit of doubt, I think it would be correct to observe that even if the rough guy is intelligent, he certainly isn't very sharp. A player, of all people, should know that when he loses his punch he will also lose his skates. When these fellows return to the mines of life in the workaday world all crippled up, it may dawn on some of them that they were exploited for a few seasons by a management that found out that roughhousing added "color" to the game and filled a few more seats with loutish fellows who get their jollies not in appreciating talent but in watching an ordinary guy take on his betters.

An interesting observation apropos of all this is that the

players with reputations for unnecessary roughness usually play for several different teams in the League during their career as tormentors. Oftentimes, as in the case of Stan Mikita whose early career found him frequently in the penalty box, a player having established himself in the League no longer feels the necessity for taking on any and all opponents. One year Keith Magnuson piled up a record of 213 minutes in the penalty box—3 hours and 55 minutes when he was of no use to the team—and that's a lot of time for a player with talent. He has been noticeably tapering off his inclination for destruction. In the same season that Magnuson watched much of the season from the penalty box Bobby Hull served a total of only 8 minutes.

Hindsight, restoring 20/20 vision, shows that Derek Sanderson of the Boston Bruins amassed a total of 118 minutes in penalties in the 1970 season, in which he played in 50 out of 76 games. A tormented opponent finally racked him up for a five-week layoff. Sanderson returned to the ice in time for the Stanley Cup playoffs and spent 72 minutes—1 hour and 12 minutes of playing time—in the penalty box while his team played shorthanded. Through the talent of their superstars, Boston won the cup in spite of playing so much of the time at a disadvantage. An interesting commentary.

In an attempt to deal with fighting, a new rule was adopted at the beginning of the 1971–72 season. The new regulation states that a third-man intervention in a scrap that is already under way gets the offender a $100 fine, plus the rest of the evening off work.

"It has stopped the mass scramble from the bench in answer to the invitation to the dance to participate in a sweater-pulling contest. It has also discouraged a lot of the fellows who didn't want to fight in the first place. Before the new rule you could start a fight knowing that help was coming quickly. Now you have to fight it out on your own, and not everybody's willing to do that." So comments Coach Billy Reay.

Keith Magnuson's reaction to the new rule was that you are still free to start something on your own.

The historic fracas in Philadelphia in December, 1971, had many fans wondering what happened to the new ruling on that occasion. It happened during a game between the Philadelphia Flyers and the St. Louis Blues. At the signal of the end of the second period the Blues Coach Al Arbour charged out on the ice to argue over the validity of a goal that the Flyers had just scored. He was so wrapped up in serving his cause that he followed the referee across the ice to the dressing-room gate. He came within range of a fan who poured beer over him. It was at this moment that the Blues on their way to the dressing room came to the rescue of their coach and went over the wall after the fan. This started a general melee into which the police entered. Everybody lost—the coach, players, fans, cops, and general public. But this was not a fight between the teams or individual players. A fiasco such as this one, which attained national attention, had only one possible violation of League rules and that was the presence of the coach on the ice. But on the other hand, the game was in recess, and the coach and the team were on their way to the dressing room.

There were conflicting reports in the press as to what exactly went on, so many readers presumed that this occasion was nothing more than a brawl between hockey teams. The Flyers were already in their dressing room by the time that the fists and debris started flying. They didn't even get to watch the battle. Moreover, they had to sit locked up in the dressing room until the fracas subsided and order had been restored in the stands, not having the faintest idea what was going on in the Spectrum. The St. Louis coach and three of his players were served papers to appear in court a month later—upon their return for another "game" with the Flyers. It might be noted that the offending fans were not arrested.

"Sometimes somebody has to step into a guy, not necessarily in anger, but to set things right," explains Magnuson. "I can think of a couple of times when I would have pounded a bum right into the ice if I had been there at the time."

One example of what Keith was referring to was Bryan Watson, then of the Philadelphia Flyers (the fifth NHL team he has played with in ten years, plus intermittent play with farm teams). Watson was usually assigned to shadow Bobby Hull. This is a tactic where the shadower doesn't even try to get the puck but simply to harass his opponent. Hull himself says that he doesn't mind a man going up and down the ice with him because that's part of the game, but when all he does is obstruct and doesn't try get on offense, then the game suffers. In one game Watson skated in behind Bobby, held his stick up before him, and slammed into him as Hull was about to shoot. Bobby went down but cracked Watson on the head as he went by. He had been harassed beyond endurance. As with Apps, so with Watson, Bobby apologized to him after the game. Watson's attitude was a threat that a long season lay ahead.

"Sanderson's another one," said Cliff Koroll. "That guy is all smugness. I always want to take a run at him."

"It's a good thing for Derek that I wasn't on the ice that time he hit Tony Esposito as he was going for a breakaway puck. I'd have broken him in half," remembered Magnuson.

THE rule in hockey is that never, under *any* circumstances, does one strike down a goaltender. Any man who will do this, even in the heat of battle, is regarded as a bum.

"The guy isn't a fighter to begin with," said Cliff. "He's always starting things when he thinks he has an advantage, and then he disappears in the crowd when the going gets rough. He's good at the cop-out."

Another example of player attitudes is that expressed by Paul Shmyr, the Black Hawk defenseman. We were discussing the roughness of some hockey players, John Ferguson of the Montreal Canadiens in particular. "No wonder Ferguson wanted to play hockey. I've cost him $200 this year already. In that final 30 seconds last night he acted up again, so I flattened him with a body block. Sure, I drew a penalty. He followed the ref and me over to the penalty box. As soon

131

as the ref reported my offense and skated away to do a face-off, Ferguson tried to hit me on the head as he reached over the glass partition and swung at me with his stick. And there went another hundred."

"When a player is getting into fights," observes Coach Billy Reay, "it usually means that he's bothering the opposition. Fights are inevitable with spirited men." After the game with Vancouver, Dan Maloney, a rookie that year making his fistic debut explained, "Maki hit me across the face with his stick as we came off the boards. I didn't wait for an explanation. I guess there wouldn't have been one anyway, so I just started swinging."

Keith Magnuson explained one of his bouts as he fulfilled his role as "policeman." "Everytime they broke it up, we'd get to talking, then somebody would start shoving and then it would start up all over again. I have to play my game, and this is part of it. I can't play the game that fans who criticize me want me to play. If the penalty minutes count up, that's just part of it. It's not that I lose control on the ice. I'm just not aware of what I'm doing at the time. In a fight on the ice, all you're conscious of is the guy you're fighting with. It's just you and him alone. I also don't think you can be overaggressive in hockey. It's part of playing the game. I jump in and intervene when I see a teammate getting a treatment. To me this is part of good team spirit. I cannot stand around when a teammate's in trouble. It's an unwritten law that you step in and help out."

Billy Reay confessed that he'd be unhappy if Mag was losing the fights. "I never encourage them to fight, but I like to see them able to take care of themselves when the occasion arises."

One of Magnuson's friends who had grown up with him recalled that he wasn't even very aggressive in the early days. "I remember him as being rather small and retiring, but always working hard at the game. We laughed at him because he practiced with weights on his skates. He was the worst shot in Saskatoon, but he was forever working on it. When we were seven or eight years old his folks wouldn't let him play on Sunday. While they were napping he'd sneak out and we'd have his gear ready for him." Persistent hammering pays off—and that's the cost of excellence. When Mag made his first goal in the National Hockey League he received an ovation as well as the puck.

The trend in hockey toward bigger and heavier men does not necessarily increase the fisticuffs or general aggression. There are simply more heavyweight bouts these days. Jerry Korab, the Black Hawks' rookie defenseman, is alternately known as "Li'l Abner," because of muscle, size, and looks. But he is also known as "King Kong" and "The Crusher"—and for good reason. With his skates on he is about 6'5" +. Complete with suit and padding he's built like an icehouse—215 pounds in the shower room.

Jerry has a few philosophical observations to make. "I soon found out that I couldn't take a run at a guy in this League like I could in Portland. If you make a mistake here, he's gone. You have to make sure you're going to hit him and take him out of the play before you take a run at him because maybe he won't be there when you arrive." Looking him over, even from across the coffee table, I knew that anyone hit by Korab ran the risk of sticking to the boards after the blow.

"The way I figure it," said Jerry, "is if they start calling you uncomplimentary names like they do me, it means that they notice that I'm out there on the ice. The rough stuff is part of the game I like. I don't feel like I'm in the game unless somebody takes me into the boards or I take someone else in for the ride. If the game gets quiet I find it sort of boring. But once somebody gets in a whack it makes everybody sharp and we go charging all over the ice."

The conclusion? There are many players who would fight in a game of shinny at night during a blizzard and when the temperature was 20 below zero, and there were no spectators. Why?

The Law of the Ice prevails: "Thou Shalt Not Back Down."

13

Pressures and Palaces

●

Of all major professional sports, hockey is the least reward-
ing financially. The Stanley Cup, hockey's championship,
great and coveted honor that it is, does not bring the champions the material gains that championships in the other
sports do. The National Football League champions receive
about $25,000 per man. The World Series-winning Pitts-
burgh Pirates received $18,000. The NBA, the major basket-
ball league, pays its champions $17,500 for winning. In order
to do this the NBA splits $700,000. The National Hockey
League pool is $777,000. Although this figure approximates

the National Basketball Association pool, the latter's rosters are smaller. Almost twice as many hockey players share a slightly larger pool.

In the NHL all salaries terminate on the last day of the regular season. From there on, players are compensated with prize money. If a star receives $78,000 for the season, it amounts to $1,000 a game in the playoffs. He's going to play at lower pay and sometimes virtually without pay should the team not go far in the playoffs. If the playoffs go to the maximum of 21 games, he earns $367 per game. For a 12-game playoff, he would receive $650 per game.

Upon learning this, some fans may react with, "650 bucks for a night's work? It takes me a month to haul in that much." The answer is, "Do you take the same risks? Do you frequently have to be put back together after a day's work or does your reassembly require only a couple of beers or a highball? Also, how many years can you expect to work on your job? Most of these players top out after twelve to fifteen years—with certain exceptions. After that, what are they prepared to do in order to make a living?

Moreover, over seven months are spent traveling and keeping irregular and outrageous hours. As an example of what a pain in the neck this can be, let's take a look at how the players live during the season. For every scheduled game away from home, the team leaves the previous night, usually after eleven o'clock. By the time they arrive in the city where the next game is to be played, bussed into the city and bedded down, it is usually around three in the morning.

Their day is free—what there is of it after having slept off the effects of night travel and late arrival. They usually have their pregame meal around three in the afternoon and arrive at the local stadium or arena around six o'clock or so. The game is over by ten o'clock. The flight home or to the next game leaves by midnight. Should there be no game the next night, the flight directly home puts the players back in their own beds at three or four o'clock in the morning.

When there are two or three days between scheduled

games, there are still frequent daily workouts. There are personal bruise and injury needs that need taking care of. Or perhaps a certain line of two wings and a center have not been scoring in recent games and they are beginning to feel the pressure of not contributing their share of points. So they meet at the arena for their own workout and the ironing out of their problems and hang-ups in plays and maneuvers. So, days off aren't always days off.

The team statistician keeps track of which front line and defensive line is on the ice when the opponents score points. If and when this falls into a regular pattern of one line being on the ice when points are scored, then there is an obvious problem that must be solved. The men get out there and work through their difficulties. If a line spends two hours or so working out the kinks in their play and leave that afternoon for the flight to the West Coast for a road trip beginning the next day, they have little time to themselves except on a flight and the middle of the next day. It's push, push, push and go, go, go through a 78-game grind over a seven-month schedule. Then for the division leaders the playoffs begin. There is no let-up.

With every team playing during the Christmas and New Year holidays this means that half the teams are away from their families at this time of year. The glamour and excitement of the game as experienced by the fans is not part of the life of the hard-working and forever-traveling professional hockey player. Then, too, how can you get yourself "psyched up" for three or four games a week for seven months? Pro football players reportedly start their hate-syndromes going six days before a game, and even then report inabilities to do so very well over a season of sixteen or so games. The hockey player has neither the opportunity nor the luxury of preparing for a game by getting himself in the proper attitude in order to produce superior play on his part.

The basketball player and the hockey player have a rootless existence during the season. Football players have it the easiest. In baseball the team stays in a city for a three-

or four-game schedule as part of a road trip that may last as long as two or three weeks. The hockey player has traveled anywhere from 10,000 to 20,000 miles and slept in a dozen different hotels, dozed in two dozen buses and airplanes in that length of time. Think about this side of it when your envy of them begins to eat you up. They're working stiffs, too.

Add to all this the fatigue and exhaustion, the new pains and pulled muscles, the constant threat of new or aggravated injuries, and the recovery from a rough game while riding a jet at midnight. Skip Thayer may say to the man complaining of a new pain, "Come on down tomorrow morning and we'll see what we can do." But until morning there is little to do but get as comfortable as possible.

At last the player arrives home and falls into bed. By the time he is up in the morning the family man finds that the kids are off to school. He is due at the arena for a treatment or a workout. Perhaps there is a home game that night. If so, he may have a nap at home, have a solid dinner around three in the afternoon, and leave again for the arena at the time the kids come home from school. Oftener than not, that night he flies with the team to their next game. He has about as much home life as an astronaut on a mission.

Thus the Black Hawks went through the grind of a 78-game 1970–71 schedule, and won the divisional championship. They next had to win the best of seven playoff games up to twenty-one games if each series were to go the full seven games through the Stanley Cup. They beat the Philadelphia Flyers four games straight. These games were played within a week with the teams shuttling back and forth between Philadelphia and Chicago. Then came a seven-game series with the New York Rangers which included a seemingly endless triple overtime game, and the usual flying back and forth between New York and Chicago.

Without a let-up, the Black Hawks then faced the Montreal Canadiens for the Stanley Cup. At first the momentum was theirs, although it took two overtime periods for them to win the opener 2–1. In that game the offense included 58 shots on the Canadien goal. With only one night's rest in between, the two teams took to the ice again and the Black Hawk momentum held as Chicago won again 5–3. But every game exacts a price: game one with its overtime meant more fatigue; in game two, Pat Stapleton's face was badly cut by a skate and Rick Foley, a rookie, had to replace him.

The series shifted to alien ice for the Black Hawks. Montreal responded to the occasion and its home fans by overtaking and beating a 2–0 Chicago lead 3–2, and this was followed by another Montreal home victory 5–2.

Things stood at 2–2 in games. It was a new series and a harder pull uphill for Chicago, who had lost its solid advantage. Nevertheless, Chicago came back with a shutout, 2–0, against a Montreal team hit by dissension. Now they were down to it. In one more game the Black Hawks could win it all—and everything seemed to be going for them. Nothing helps a team's spirits like a shutout, and Tony Esposito had provided just that. Chicago took over the lead and held on at 3–2, but Montreal took hold. Frank Mahovlich tied it 3–3, and his brother Pete plunged the Black Hawks into disappointment with a fourth Canadien goal, and suddenly the teams were even again.

And so it came full circle. The Chicago ice, the press with its cameras and typewriters, the Chicago players skating their circles in the familiar arena as they had that first day of training among the cameras and writers of September. But now the stadium did not echo with emptiness, it exploded with the sounds of fans packed to the rafters. And now the Black Hawks were sharing their ice with that one team among all the NHL contenders that had stuck out the long, eventful, grinding season to arrive at this lonely point were everything was at stake and where only one more chance was left to decide the Ultimate Winner.

The opening formalities took place—everything in its place—and the game started.

Again Chicago came on with a rush. Quickly, in the first

period they took a 2–0 lead. They skated well and checked hard, going all out, for there would be no tomorrow. They could not be denied.

But they were. The second period began. Jacques Lemaire scored on a long shot and suddenly Montreal was back in the game. The Black Hawks now seemed to be fading. Desperately they fought to hold their lead, but Henri Richard moved in with a goal and it was 2–2 as the period ended.

The third period began and it was a new game—a game that was eighteen minutes too long and therefore a season that was eighteen minutes too long. By the third minute of the third period, the last of the year's energies and effort were expended. Actually, for both teams there was nothing left to give. They struggled for that vital extra burst that could yield just that one more all-taking goal. Up and down the ice the players went, behind the goal, into the boards, checking, passing, driving and being driven, sweating streams and gulping for breath, and not quite putting it together. The game ground on to what seemed might be a tie and the need for overtime. Two minutes were left when suddenly, in a last burst of energy, Henri Richard turned Keith Magnuson's fllank. Keith stretched for him and slipped. Desperately he threw his stick after the puck and just missed it. Richard barreled in just to the crease where Tony Esposito was trying to last out the last mile. Richard moved to the right, Esposito lunged to close the angle, but Richard pushed a little backhand shot, popping the puck past Tony—and that was it, 3–2. The Cup belonged to Montreal.

Keith Magnuson tried to take the blame personally— "He got away from me. I'm to blame."—but I wonder if that is true. Ninety-five and two-thirds games had taken their toll. Neither team had ten watts of energy left by that time. It's a toss-up miracle that either team could win under such conditions. The same reasons and excuses could have been used for the Canadiens if the final game had turned out in the Black Hawks' favor.

139

In spite of the grinding nature of a season's competitive play for high stakes these men do not become machines, although I suspect that there are times when they begin to wonder about this themselves.

After the final and deciding game for the Stanley Cup, Ken Dryden, the Canadien's goalie, stood in the dressing with a brand-new four-stitch cut on his chin and an ugly red spot on his breastbone. He had stopped a 100-mile-an-hour shot sent off by Dennis Hull. Scared by the effects of his own shot, Dennis was upset. "That's the first time I've ever done that," he lamented.

Earlier in the season, when he was out on the ice alone practicing his slap shot, I watched him work out. I was impressed and astonished at the shots he was making. My first thought was of the goalie who was faced with deflecting one of these fireballs. "Before every game I stand on the blue line and say to myself, 'I hope I don't hurt a goalie tonight,'" he said.

I suppose a goalie must not dare think of the possibility of getting hit. Bobby Hull says that when Dennis is cranked up and lets go, there is no goalie who can stop the shot except by luck and accident. "It'll be past him before he can make a move." Dennis himself says that in past years he had been wild with his shots, and even more dangerous. "Besides that," he added, "I have to be careful not to overskate, not to drive too far down the wing and make the angle harder to shoot. I have also had my troubles on defense."

Coach Billy Reay commented that the pressure on Dennis was tremendous at first because he was the kid brother to the most explosive player and scorer the game has ever known. "So much was expected of him that he tried too hard to do well."

"Wild as my shots are sometimes," remarks Dennis, "my consolation is that it makes goalies nervous—but I don't like to hurt a man."

He is but one of many hockey players who has not lost his humanity.

14

The Via Dollarosa

●

For when the One Great Scorer comes
To write against your name,
He marks not that you won or lost,
But how you played the Game.

This noble sentiment was penned nearly fifty years ago by Grantland Rice, the most famous sportswriter of that day. Today's sports fan knows that the day has come for this to be rewritten, for Social Darwinism—the survival of the fittest—

in sports no longer truly prevails. Today it reads more accurately from a parody or paraphrase of this quote:

For when the One Great Scorer comes
(A father image for the Internal Revenue Service),
To write against your name
(With no natural resources depletion allowance),
He marks not that you won or lost
(What counts are the computer statistics on performance),
But how you played the Game
(And for *how much* you played the Game).

It goes almost without saying that you get paid more for compiling a superior statistic record as well as winning more games than you lose. The pressure is really on a player when he's out there on the ice, for he knows among other things that if a goal is scored against the team when he's out there that *somebody* marked this down on a clipboard. If this happens regularly or too often he is not surprised if he slides down the totem pole of rank and excellence in the minds of coaching and management.

On offense, if his line is not producing goals, this means that the center and the two wings had better arrange to conduct a few trysts, or practice sessions, on the ice all by themselves before the statistician (First Assistant to the One Great Scorer), presents his computerized conclusions to the higher powers in the coach's office or upstairs before the managerial throne of grace.

When either the offensive or defensive units are not going well, for instance, there is a marked absence of the repartee and humor one expects among hard-working comrades. There is no whistling past graveyards with these men. Nor is there cutting down of telephone lines to avoid bad news. The cure is always analysis, correction, and plain hard work. Only when this is done can the vital team balance be restored physically and psychologically.

The mistakes involved can often be small, such as starting off on the wrong foot and losing a step. On the higher levels of hockey, as in any other highly professional endeavor in either sports, the arts, or in research, it is most often a slight matter that has created the impasse. This is especially noticeable with the golf professional in that highly individualized sport. The slightest change in stance or movement will frequently throw his entire game out of cadence. In hockey a line that is in trouble talks the problem over, sometimes working for hours to learn why things have not been going well for them. As in any other endeavor, when things are going well, don't dissect it. Leave it alone.

Writing of these matters recalls the many times that I watched three men work out their offensive play over and over again, unkinking the line of efficiency and power. It seems to me that the center usually gets the blame—and almost always takes it. Stan Mikita's instruction to his young wings illustrates the point: "Keep your stick on the ice. Skate like hell. It's up to me to get the puck to you."

This is the cost of excellence.

Last year a certain Toronto player became unhappy and asked to be traded. He had been suffering from acute depressions and underwent some psychiatric treatment on his own. There are many other situations similar to this appearing among professional hockey players. The intense pressures under which these young men live and operate are created by the heavy schedule, the constant cross-country travel, the rugged body contact, and the constant movement on the ice.

Midway in the season there is a four-day break to make way for the All-Star Game, but this is no break for the forty players involved in that annual extravaganza. During this time there are also League meetings, coach's meetings, and resultant trades and rumors of trades. All this is highly unsettling to men who are getting ready for the big push to the playoffs.

Players testify that hockey is more physically draining than any other sport. Even so, I have not been able to find a shred of evidence that these men have pep pills given to them, nor do they have the time between games to "psyche" themselves up for a "big one." I must confess that after seeing the Black Hawks lose a close game or one in which they were simply outplayed because of what I took to be fatigue, I had to "psyche" myself into going into the dressing room after the game. The moment I walked in I could immediately feel them going straight down into the depths. Collision, violence, and fear of injury are not really factors. The real danger is getting tired. I have seen it markedly after a game. Frequently it could be perceived before a game, and I would know that tonight was not going to be a good night on the ice for them.

I asked various players where they were going after the final series. The answers were always much the same: "Me? I'm going where there isn't any ice, crowds, dressing rooms, whoop-la or national anthems or some guy with a pencil and clipboard marking down my sins for me. I'm going where I don't have to be nice to jock-sniffers and brown-nosers. Sand, sun, and surf for me and the whole family. I haven't anything left." When one player confided to me that he was going to Greece and the Aegean Islands for a holiday because of his interest in archeology I reminded him that even that far-off age had statisticians and bookkeepers, too, as evidenced by the mass of inscriptions. "Yes, I know," he replied, "but they aren't on me."

It would be presumptuous and stupid of me to say that "my season" with the Black Hawks was as grueling and fatiguing for me as it was for them. Usually it was fun, for all the hard work. But there were more times than I liked when getting to the heart of the story I've been trying to write was as difficult as getting a puck past Tony Esposito into the Black Hawk net.

The spirit and principle of training camp permeates all of hockey. I think that hockey is the most secretive of all sports. The left hand never finds out what the right hand is doing. Trying to find out what's going on is as difficult as finding out the private lives of nineteenth-century Victorian personalities. One always suspects that it's there, like merchandise in a hardware store—around some place if you can just find it. I sometimes felt a great deal like the guy who played the piano in a brothel for two years before he knew what was going on upstairs. In time I began to hear the shoes drop and got the feeling that someone else had been had.

The game is beginning to lose its innocence. The salaries of the players are slowly and gradually coming to light. Young lawyers, seeking to make a mark in the sports world and believing that too little is made of the value of the professional athlete, have moved in to help (for a fee) the players receive as much as players in other sports for a comparable performance. The hockey boys are having their moment of truth these days since they are beginning to find out that in the national basketball leagues reserve players receive more salary than topflight hockey stars.

"They pull this old wheeze on you that 'I can't give in to you or I'd have to face eighteen other guys and would lose the respect of the team.' "—so stated a holdout. "It's a matter of pride, now. I cannot any more sign a contract that's for less than what I know I'm worth to the club."

Another commented that he had served his apprenticeship for two years. "This year is the chance for the biggest salary increase that I can ever hope for. This is my only chance to make it, so it's all or nothing this time around."

This kind of talk and conviction is something that has been added to the prescription that goes into producing a first-rank hockey player. They never used to talk about their salaries, probably because they were so embarrassed at the ridiculous figure. Even the eighth-round draft choice in pro football receives more than the top rookie in hockey.

As far as anybody can find out, hockey has only one $100,000 a year man—Bobby Hull. There are several players in the NHL who are up with him in scoring and yet they don't make a third of this figure, except for three or four of them. The roosts are fast filling up with returned chickens in management's henhouse. Player's representatives and agents are talking in terms of $40,000, $50,000, and $60,000 for their clients. Management isn't talking, presumably because they are getting slack-jawed with the turning of tables and are faced with making up a new list of reasons why this salary range is unrealistic. The only answers to come up so far are "We know the economics of hockey; the players do not," or "We deal with people who know the business." All of which reminds me of one of the classic lines from a Gilbert and Sullivan operetta: "It's one of the happiest characteristics of this happy country that its official utterances are invariably regarded as unanswerable."

Trying to look at big-time sports in perspective and with some balance, one can see hockey as part of the social and business phenomenon that is the United States of America in the last third of this century. The pall of big business which has made the extravaganzas possible is beginning to affect our Canadian brothers through its inevitable dehumanization. Even the young executives of today hardly know from day to day what conglomerate they are working for. This is a familiar picture to the ancient history buff who sees in the expansion and development and promotion of big-time sports the same process that went on in the Roman Empire. The custom in those days was to finance the arenas by public subsidy. They also had an advantage in that the Emperor Divine could pass the responsibility for the success of any arena to a "friend" who was a political enemy, thus helping his opponent keep his capital so distributed that he could not assist in financing resistance to his clique. Now, there's an idea that hasn't been tried in our society.

Eventually these practices, plus simply the giantism that resulted, degenerated Roman entertainment into second-class burlesque. American sports may not be too far away from that now. It is fairly obvious in wrestling and boxing already. A faint glimmer of what may come can be seen in the rerun of collections of incidents in pro football that are truly funny. It is becoming a spoof.

It seems to me that baseball, basketball, and now football are becoming highly stylized. If these sports do not deteriorate into burlesque and suffer the fate of boxing and wrestling, they may take the other extreme and metamorphose in a stylized theater, such as Japanese Kabuki drama, where everybody knows always where the bodies are buried and how the story will come out.

In football, as an example, it is becoming almost easier for the sports fan to predict the forthcoming play than it is for the defense. One of the virtues of hockey is that this will never be possible. The very nature of hockey makes classical plays and classicized behavior incapable of being developed. All sports are beginning to suffer from overexposure on television. This is not likely to happen to hockey because of its sheer unpredictability of movement and action. So it may outlast all other sports in their present form.

At least big-time management and ownership see it this way, and for these very good reasons. Let's see how expansion is getting on in the NHL. There are two more teams added to the League for the 1972–73 season—Atlanta and Long Island. Other franchises will be added in 1974–75 and still more later, so that by 1980 there will be a twenty-four team National Hockey League. The understanding is that each existing team may protect fifteen players and two goalies. (Atlanta and Long Island will be "stocked" by nineteen players and two goalies each.)

This isn't the end of expansion. Here we go again, as in the days of American and National Football League competition and finally amalgamation. The process is already advanced in baseball. It may take awhile longer for these steps to be reached by hockey. What is happening, however, is the formation of the World Hockey Association; so, fans and players, hang on to your hats, we're off.

If the WHA comes through, as is expected in most quarters, a goodly number of players now wearing NHL uniforms may jump to the new league in the next year or two. There have already been wars and rumors of wars that the new league has been trying to entice top stars, including a million-dollar offer to Bobby Hull.

Derek Sanderson of the Boston Bruins claims that he received a generous offer from the WHA. His reaction to the new league was that every NHL team has underpaid players and that if you're a young guy and have a wife and kids, you aren't going to stay around for $20,000 when you can get $60,000 somewhere else.

Bobby Hull said, "Those players who want to jump will have an opportunity to make a little more money, but they'll have a tough road. If the new league gets going they might entice some NHL players. They might even get 25 or 30 percent. But who they're interested in is something else. Quite a few players they might be interested in probably won't be interested in them. And then there will be a lot of players who will be interested but won't be invited."

Glen Sather of the New York Rangers thinks that if another league comes bidding for services, the players will all have a chance to be individuals again—to sell their bodies. "If you don't listen you're crazy. It doesn't mean you'll go, but you've got to listen." (Now that fellow has had a recent moment of truth in which he has few illusions about what a hockey club wants of him.)

In general, according to a press survey on the subject, the players agree that the presence of a rival league would raise the salary level in the NHL, but they were divided on how many of their colleagues would be lured away. The consensus was that the fringe and older players in the NHL and scores of minor leaguers would be the most likely candidates to sign with the new World Hockey League.

With due credit to the NHL it must be stated that they have an excellent pension plan. Their players have the prestige of belonging to the best league of its kind in the world, and they have the status of having already made it. Some NHL players say that a move in that direction would have to be motivated by more than a salary raise and assurance that it would not be a one-year shot and no security.

Others believe that the superstars won't take the chance and that the war will be for the younger men and not for the established stars. "I'm satisfied with my salary," said Bernie Parent, currently with Toronto. "Why go somewhere you don't know what's going to happen? I know some guys who are unhappy in the NHL, so they might as well take a chance and go with the new league. The league will get off the ground but how long it will last is another question."

There are several that believe that any NHL player who receives a good offer will make the move. "Of course they'll take players from the NHL. Money talks. Besides that, it opens the doors for borderline players."

A California Seal player said that he had been advised to take the best possible deal and don't stick with a team or a league through loyalty alone because they won't do that for you.

And so it goes. Everybody waits for history to repeat itself in hockey as it has done in baseball, football, and basketball. And it probably will. One cannot help but wonder where all these new teams will hold franchises. It is known that in the planned NHL expansion that within seven or eight years there will be NHL hockey teams in Baltimore, Cleveland, Kansas City, Washington, Indianapolis, San Diego, Denver, and probably Portland or Dallas, although in the latter case they are a farm club of the Chicago Black Hawks.

Regardless of all the factors that operate against the individual in any enterprise that has the size and scope of big time sports, I found the hockey players to be men who knew the cost of excellence in the development of their art and skill. They paid the price regularly and willingly and without complaint. I found that these young Canadian athletes have not lost their love of The Game in spite of its being developed into big business with all the ballyhoo and whoop-la of the American Sports Extravaganza.

In view of this, and particularly considering his statement just quoted, more recent news of Bobby Hull has taken on a heavily ironic significance.

Rumors and rumblings of Bobby Hull's courtship by the WHA began during the mid-season of 1971–72. This was before any announcements proclaiming the capture of several NHL players were made. At the time, "official sources" —management and press—discounted the possibilities of Hull's moving because of the considerable amount of money that would have to be raised. Of course, there was also the belief that since Hull had only played for the Black Hawks, for him to play anywhere else had become unthinkable. On June 27, the official news was out that Bobby had been signed to be player-coach of the new Winnipeg team, beginning at training camp in the fall of 1972. This gives credence to the many bits of floating anxiety, known as rumors, concerning the brewing defections of other stars and superstars.

With such arrangements as these being made with the development of the WHA and the expansion of the NHL into Atlanta and Long Island, it has certainly become a players' market. Will it end with a bang or a whimper? All of us are wondering and waiting as the biggest game of musical chairs over talent and expansion that has ever been known in organized sports goes on.

These new player-coaches, such as John Mackenzie and Bobby Hull, are about to find new moments of truth over the problems of management. It's a great experience changing places in a boat in midstream. Educational, too.

15

Happy Returns

●

Even in the soggy heat of late August I began thinking ice hockey and my return to the opening of training camp. I was curious about what my reception might be this year, now that I had the advantage of acquaintance and familiarity. It turned out to be an interesting comparison. The previous year I had entered the Chicago Stadium with considerable apprehension and anxiety. This time I arrived full of anticipation, yet with a slight reservation, not really knowing whether or not I would be welcomed sincerely or simply recognized as still being among the camp followers.

Monday, September 13 arrived for everybody, but in a special way for the Chicago Black Hawks, the press, the radio and television media—and me. Today was the opening of the training camp for the 1971–72 season. Although I believed that I was prepared for nearly any kind of response —positive or negative—upon my arrival, I certainly did not expect the reception that I received. Even the security police doorman greeted me with a handshake. Considerably buoyed up by this greeting, I went directly to the business office to park my luggage and announce my return to the fields of battle. There, too, I was welcomed in such a way that I knew I was picking up where I left off last spring—at the Coke cooler in Murphy's office helping myself, as usual.

After exchanging reports on our respective summers I made my way to the rink. There were my friends skating round and round. They looked as though they might have been there all summer. The only immediately perceptible change was their summer tan plus a rested and refreshed look. I remembered how fatigued and exhausted these men looked during the playoff games for the Stanley Cup competition last March and April. The 78-game season had taken its toll so strongly that I wondered at the time how these men could hold together during the last and most important effort. I also recalled that last year's Stanley Cup finals were eighteen minutes too long.

I thought upon these things as I went down the aisle to the gate the team came through on their way to and from the locker room. As soon as I showed up at ice edge the players stopped skating their endless oval and pulled up to shake hands, apparently genuinely glad to see me. Questions and queries about the book came fast, plus some kidding about "Haven't you had enough yet?"; "Are you going to suit up this year?" and "Where's your skates?"

The coach skated by and stopped for a brief greeting. His arrival coincided with the departure of the cluster at the gate and their return to the Endless Round. What had I been worried about? I went down to the training room.

As I walked into the "infirmary" (I suppose it should be called), I greeted Skip Thayer and Lou Vargas with the announcement and explanation that I was out making sick calls and thought that I should start out with them.

"Is it intensive care that you want?" asked Skip.

"He'll need it if he comes into the stockroom and steals pucks for his boys back in the parish," warned Lou.

The voice from under the sheet on the training table urged the handlers to get with it. The patient was Jim Pappin.

"Last year it was Bell's palsy, wasn't it?" I recalled. "And now a shoulder problem, I see. There must be a difference between a golf swing and a slap shot, what?" I diagnosed.

"Gonna be around this year, too?" asked Jim, ignoring my guess. "I'm waiting for that book."

"So am I," I answered. "I can hardly wait to read how it all comes out."

"You mean, you don't know?" asked Skip.

"Not yet," I commented mysteriously, although I didn't really know, yet.

It was as though I had not been away for five months, and this was most heartening. The players were filing into the locker room now that the first workout was over. Lunch was ready. The next event of old home week came up.

To me, this was a most relaxed affair as far as I was concerned although I picked up the climate of general anxiety that pervaded the room. However, this year I was able to discern that it was specifically generated by the rookies, the young men with the uncertain futures. There were many unrecognized faces, new recruits making their first bid for an NHL berth. They looked at me as curiously as had last year's crop, but this time I understood it because I was a last year's rookie myself. Introducing myself to those rookies who came to the table on either side, I explained who I was and what I was doing there. I detected a faint relief on some faces when it was realized that I wasn't part of the judge's court team-wise or press-wise.

The tension was contagious. I picked up the vague hint that a couple of last year's rookies weren't sure that they wouldn't be shipped out at the end of training camp. Two weeks later it came about that their anxieties and suspicions were well founded: two were returned to a farm club for "more seasoning," which in coach and management language means "We don't feel that he has quite enough talent to make it with us." This reminds me of the shade of difference between "failing" and "not yet successful."

Nor was I stared down suspiciously by the sports reporters, but greeted warmly. Of course, by now my tentative or defensive attitude had already been completely melted by returning to training camp. There were no more rivers to cross. This was good.

The afternoon workout included scrimmage. Everyone was somewhat surprised by this announcement because heretofore a couple of days of workout had preceded the hard body contact of scrimmage. As usual the rookies were trying to melt the ice with their bursts of speed. They did everything in their power to convince themselves—and others—that they might well be the find of the season and the sport's next superstar although there wasn't a one of them who wouldn't settle just for being squad member.

Early in the scrimmage one of the anonymous rookies managed to score two goals within a minute. This created a minor flutter and stir among the scrimmagers. It was noticed that it was the last time that he got within 30 feet of the goal while still on his skates for the whole afternoon. This was managed so quietly and efficiently that I'm still not sure who administered the body checks.

One began to sense that the Black Hawks were going to start the season with the same squad that almost won the Stanley Cup the previous spring. From this an educated hunch emerged that if they didn't make it this year then it would be difficult to determine who would be traded to one of the two expansion clubs and who would possibly try to jump to the new World Hockey League. Nothing whatsoever was said or indicated by anyone within my earshot certainly, and I rather felt that there was a quiet ground swell of unstated opinion that the old familiar game of musical chairs may begin next year. Everybody wore that undefinable look of unconcern on their faces which tried to convey to the other fellow that they alone knew where the body was hidden. A worrisome and anxious business, indeed.

Looking backward over the days and weeks that I went through the learning process and finding out what hockey was all about and how it worked in the big-time setting—to my surprise, the book was easier to accomplish than I could possibly have hoped for. It didn't turn out as expected, though. The major problem was keeping neutral and maintaining what is called objectivity. The players made it too easy for me to become personal friends with them.

Fortunately, most of the book had been experienced and recorded before chauvinism set in. In trying to keep up with hockey through the newspaper sport pages during those periods when it was not possible to be with the team, I was totally dependent upon East Coast reporting. It was easy to become convinced that the Chicago Black Hawks were regarded as a second-class gang for geographical reasons alone. Their home ice was on the west side of the Hudson River. Consequently the eastern press, in reporting the losses of eastern teams in the NHL to Chicago (while playing there, of course), invariably implied that the visiting team was not at its best because they (1) suffered from the bends and their blood became carbonated when they played so far away from home or (2) the hostile natives swarming down out of their trees made it impossible to play under such primitive conditions.

Oftentimes in scanning the sport sections I would look for news of the Black Hawks—successes on the ice, misfortunes of injuries to the players, masterly trading by management. Not a word. The sins of editorial omission seemed to imply that the Black Hawks were semiliterate primitives and that the team was loaded with hockey bullies and thugs. One even got the idea sometimes that Bobby Hull, of all athletes, was a cloak-and-dagger man who thrived on bully tactics. It was often implied, it seemed to me, that the Hawks were called a "physical" team because they lacked the talent to play true hockey. This is hard on all us midwesterners who are required by the chances and changes of life to live on the East Coast. This is part of what I mean by losing one's objectivity.

In a word I was "hooked," not by the game alone nor its dazzling extravaganzas and impromptu battle royals but mostly by the players. They know the cost of excellence and they pay it every time they skate out on the ice for the evening's struggle.

157

Index

Ramsay, Jack, 100
Reay, Billy, 31–32, 34–36, 50, 124, 129, 132, 140
Richard, Henri, 139
Romanchyk, Larry, 89
Ruck, Don, 12

Sample, Johnny, 118
Sanderson, Derek, 129, 131, 148
Sather, Glen, 148
Shmyr, Paul, 131
Skov, Art, 63–66, 89
St. Louis Blues, 130
Stanley, Frederick Arthur, Lord of Preston, 17–18
Stapleton, Pat, 34, 57, 59, 62, 112, 138

Thayer, Skip, 52–54, 63, 66, 69–70, 84–86, 137, 153
Tkaczuk, Walter, 55
Toronto Maple Leafs, 123

Vancouver, 68
Vargas, Lou, 55–56, 69–70, 85–86, 107–108, 153
Vass, George, v
Verdi, Bob, v, 31
Vezina Trophy, 51

Walsh, Ed, v
Watson, Bryan, 119, 131
White, Bill, 52, 62, 92, 108, 112